Presented

to _____

from _____

date _____

CREATION
(Seymour Fleishman)

A Treasure House BOOK OF CHILDREN'S BIBLE STORIES

Text by Edward G. Finnegan

Paintings by Ben Stahl

Illustrations by Seymour Fleishman

Book Design by Charles Bozett

Consolidated Book Publishers

CHICAGO • NEW YORK

Contents

CONTENTS

CONTENTS

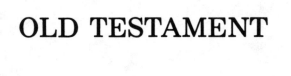

OLD TESTAMENT

Noah's Boat

GOD made the earth. Colorful birds filled the air, gentle lions and happy lambs ran across green valleys and up strong mountains. Then God put man on this earth to be happy. Man should have thanked God and loved Him, but instead man forgot God. Men began to commit more and more crimes and became so bad that one day God said sorrowfully:

"I am sorry that I made man and the earth and the animals. I will destroy them all."

But one man had remembered how good God was. His name was Noah. Noah lived quietly with his wife and his three sons, Shem, Ham, and Japheth, and their wives. Other people thought Noah was a fool because he believed in God and would not join in the evil men did. But God knew that Noah was a good man and one day He said to Noah:

"Men have filled the earth with evil. I am going to destroy them all. But I will save you and your family. I want you to make an ark. Make it from wood and seal the cracks with tar. It should be 450 feet long, 75 feet wide, and 45 feet high and have a large door in the side. Put a window in the ark, right below the roof, and put three decks inside—bottom, middle, and top."

Noah must have wondered why God would want him to make a boat so large. Why, Noah's house could fit into such a boat a hundred times over! But God continued:

"I am going to send a flood to cover the earth. But you and your family will be safe inside the ark. And I want you to put two of every kind of animal into the ark. And take enough food of all kinds to last you a long time."

Noah and his sons began work right away, chopping down trees, herding animals together, clearing the field where the boat would stand. The women of the family prepared great amounts of food.

Of course, all this activity made many people curious. They would

13

pass by every day and ask:

"What are you doing, Noah?"

"Building a boat," he would say.

"A boat! What do you want a boat in the middle of a field for?"

"There is going to be a flood," Noah would answer.

"Oh, is that so, Noah? Who told you that?"

"God did."

"Imagine that! God told Noah there is going to be a flood." They would wink at each other and walk down the road laughing at the top of their voices.

But Noah continued his work. Each day the boat grew in size. And each day people would come to make fun of Noah:

"Better hurry, Noah! Look at that cloud coming!" And they would point at a tiny white cloud in the sky.

At last the boat was finished, and God told Noah to herd all the animals into the boat. Noah did as he was told. He and his sons pushed and shoved the animals into the boat—cows and sheep and lions and birds, two of every kind of animal. The noise inside the boat was deafening, with cows mooing, lions roaring, and parrots squawking.

Then God said, "Go aboard the ark with your family. In seven days I will make it rain forty days and forty nights. I will destroy evil mankind."

And it happened as God said it would. On the seventh day Noah and his sons heard the rain on the roof, soft taps at first, then stronger and stronger, splattering, storming, as if the sky itself were splashing against the ship. Outside, voices screamed, "Flood! Deluge!"

Suddenly the ship shook—the walls stretched and screeched. The ark rose slowly, higher and higher, until it bobbed on the water high above the field where Noah had built it.

The rain continued until the highest mountains disappeared under the water. And all living things outside the ark were destroyed. Only Noah was left, and his family and the animals with him. It rained for forty days and nights and then the world outside the ark was quiet.

Noah opened the window and let a dove fly outside. The bird flew back and forth but could not find any land to rest on. So it returned and Noah put out his hand and took it back into the ark.

"We must wait," Noah told his family.

Seven days later, Noah let the dove fly out again. This time the dove did not return until the evening—and in its beak it held a new olive branch.

"The water is going down now," Noah said. "We will soon be able to leave the ark."

Noah waited another seven days and again opened the window and let

the dove fly out. The dove never returned. Noah now knew it was safe to leave the ark. He opened the big door and looked out. The land was dry!

God called to Noah, "Come out of the ark and bring your family and the animals."

Shouting for joy, Noah and his family ran from the ark. All the animals tumbled out after them.

Nearby Noah built a small altar and offered a sacrifice of thanksgiving to God.

God was pleased with the sacrifice and said to Noah, "The earth is yours. I will never again destroy the earth by flood. I promise this to you and to all the people who come after you. Look—in the sky—see the sign of my promise!"

Noah and his family looked up and there, arched across the sky—green, blue, yellow, red—was the sign of God's promise—the rainbow!

16

The Tower of Babel

AFTER the great flood, Noah's family grew and grew until there were a great many people on earth. And some of the people began to say to each other:

"There are too many people here. Soon we won't have enough food for everybody."

"Yes, we'll all starve!"

"We must move to another place."

And so a great number of people joined together for the journey. They folded their tents, gathered all their things, and packed them on their camels. Then one morning they started walking across the desert towards the east where the sun was coming up. They walked for many weeks until the desert stopped and they saw a vast green plain before them. That place is called Babylonia now, but they called it the land of Shinar then. The people were very proud of themselves.

"Look!" they exclaimed. "Just look at what we have found!"

"Now we can eat as we like. Do anything we want to!"

"What fools those other people were not to come with us!"

They talked almost as if they had made the land that they had found. They forgot completely about God. They forgot that God had made the whole earth—even the land of Shinar. No one even thought of thanking God for showing them this place where the grass was so green and where the rivers flowed.

The people began building a city. Someone discovered how to make bricks. Of course, they had a great celebration because of that. They were so proud of themselves. They danced and sang and shouted as loud as they could:

"We are the greatest people on earth!"

"There is no one like us!"

And they began to make plans. After they built all their brick

houses, they said:

"We must do something that no one has ever done before."

"Yes, we must make a name for ourselves."

"What can we do?"

"Let's build a tower."

"A tower? What good is a tower?"

"Not an ordinary tower. But a tower so tall that it will reach right into heaven! When people see something like that they will say, 'My, what great people—to make a tower so high.' "

"Yes—a tower! A tower into heaven!"

So they began to build. They made millions of bricks and began laying them one on another. Every day they worked—men sweating and bosses yelling.

"Hurry up there! Don't you want the world to know how great a people we are!"

"Straighten that line of bricks! This is the greatest building ever!"

And the tower grew until the men working near the top were actually in the clouds.

But God saw all this happening. He sees everything that happens on

earth. And He said:

"These people have gone too far. They are too proud. If they finish this tower they will think there is nothing they cannot do. I will confuse their tongues."

The next day work continued on the tower. But something strange happened. The bosses were yelling the same way they always did—but the men did not obey them. Instead, they stopped working and looked at each other. They could not understand what the bosses were saying! And the men began to talk to each other about this strange language the bosses were using and—the men could not understand *each other!* Everyone was talking a different language! They screamed at each other—but no one understood. So they grew angry and began fighting. What an uproar in the whole city! All they did was fight. Finally the fighting became too much and the people began to move away from that place, scattering in all directions.

Their unfinished tower was called the Tower of Babel, because "Babel" means "confusion" and it was at the tower that God confused the people who thought they were so great.

Two People Who Laughed

ABRAM was born in Ur. Ur was a town not very far from where some people tried to build the Tower of Babel. Abram grew up in Ur and married a beautiful girl there. Her name was Sarai.

But Abram did not live his whole life in Ur. He moved with his family to a place called Haran, which is about six hundred miles north of Ur. That is a long distance to move, but they traveled the whole time near a beautiful river called the Euphrates. So the trip must have been pleasant. Then Abram had to move from Haran, too, because one day God said to him:

"I want you to leave Haran and go to a place that I will show you. I will make you the father of a great nation. I will bless you and make you famous."

Abram thought these words were strange. He had a large ranch filled with cattle and many men worked for him. But he never imagined that he would be famous. And Sarai could not have a baby. Abram was seventy-five years old and Sarai was almost as old. So how could Abram become the father of a nation?

But God told him to go and Abram obeyed. God led Abram to a country to the south. It is called Palestine today, but it was known as Canaan then. Abram settled there and was a very successful rancher.

Abram always remembered what God had said. But God did not talk to him again for a long time. And Abram wondered if he really would be father of a nation or famous. After all, he was getting older and nothing was happening.

But one night God appeared to Abram in his tent and Abram asked:

"My Lord, what is it that you are going to give me? I have no children. When I die I will have to

21

give everything I own to one of the men who works for me because I have no children to give my possessions to."

"That is not true," God said. "You will have your own child....Come outside."

Abram went outside his tent with God. It was a very clear night. The sky was deep blue and stars were scattered over it as far as Abram could see. God said:

"Look up at the sky and count the stars."

"But that is impossible," Abram said. "There are so many."

"That is how numerous your family will be. Your children's children and then their children. And on and on. Your family will be as hard to count as the stars."

Abram was astounded. But he believed what God told him.

Later, God said to Abram, "I will make a pact with you. I will make you the father of many nations. You will no longer be called Abram—which means 'noble father.' You will now be called Abraham. That means 'father of many nations.' There will be kings in your family. I will give to them all of the land of Canaan to be theirs forever."

"And what must I do?" asked Abraham.

"You will be my people and I will be your God."

"I will do everything you tell me."

"And Sarai, your wife—you will now call her Sarah, which means 'princess.' I will bless her and she will have your baby."

Abraham laughed. He thought to himself, "This is hard to believe. I'm one hundred years old and Sarah is ninety. Are we going to have a baby at our age?"

God said, "It will be as I tell you. And you will name the baby Isaac

because you laughed and Isaac means 'laughter.' "

Some time later Abraham was sitting at the door of his tent. It was the hottest part of the day and he was trying to cool himself. He looked up and saw three men standing near the tent. Abraham got up and ran to them.

"Don't pass by, friends," he called. "Here, come under the shade of this tree. I'll bring some water and food and you can refresh yourselves. It's too hot to continue walking."

"Thank you," the men said, "that would be fine."

Abraham ran into the tent.

"Sarah. Sarah, quick! Get some bread ready. We have three visitors."

Then he ran to the corral and chose one of his best calves.

"Here," he told one of his workers, "prepare a fine meal with this calf."

Everyone hurried back and forth getting the meal. When everything was ready, Abraham brought the meal to the three men who were relaxing under the tree.

"Thank you. Thank you," they said and began to eat.

"Where is Sarah, your wife?" one of them asked.

"She's in the tent," Abraham answered.

"We will visit you next year. Sarah will have a son by then."

Inside the tent, Sarah was listening. When she heard what the visitors said she laughed. "How can I have a baby," she thought to herself. "I'm ninety years old." The visitors heard her laugh and said:

"Why did Sarah laugh? Is there anything that God cannot do? We mean what we say. We will come again next year at this time. And Sarah will have a son!"

Sarah called out from the tent, "I didn't laugh."

"Oh yes, you did! And your son's name will be Isaac—because you laughed." The visitors finished their meal and left.

And it happened just as the visitors told them it would. During the next year Sarah had a baby boy and Abraham named him Isaac.

Now Abraham and Sarah had a good reason to laugh.

23

The Sacrifice of Isaac

ABRAHAM! Abraham!" God called. Abraham roused himself from sleep. "Yes, Lord?"

"Take your son, Isaac—your only son. I know how you love him. Take him to the land of Moriah right away."

"Why, Lord?" Abraham asked.

"I want you to sacrifice Isaac. I will show you a mountain in the land of Moriah. You will make a burnt offering of Isaac there."

God disappeared and Abraham was alone. He felt as if he had had a nightmare. God wanted him to kill Isaac. Abraham and Sarah had waited so many years for a child and they had only one—Isaac. And now God wanted Isaac as a sacrifice.

A sacrifice! Abraham shuddered at the thought. How often he had taken the best lamb from his flock, killed it, and burned it on an altar. He always made this offering to God. And now...now God wanted his best lamb of all—Isaac—for a sacrifice.

Abraham woke up Sarah and told her what God had asked. They both cried in each other's arms until morning.

But God had asked for this sacrifice, and Abraham knew he must obey, no matter how much it hurt. He woke up Isaac and two servants.

"Come! We must make a journey. Get dressed, Isaac. And you two men—chop some wood and put a saddle on the donkey. We will leave right away."

Isaac must have wondered why his mother kissed him so much and hugged him so tightly.

"We'll be back soon, mother."

"Yes—yes, my son," she answered, and tears rolled down her face.

"Come, Isaac," Abraham called. "God wants me to make a sacrifice. We must get started."

They traveled three days before

God pointed out a mountain in the distance. Abraham turned to his servants.

"Wait here with the donkey," he said. "The boy and I will go to that mountain over there. We will make the sacrifice and then return."

Abraham took the wood and strapped it onto Isaac's back. He carried the stone for making fire and the knife himself. They walked to the mountain.

"Father?" Isaac said.

"Yes, Isaac?"

"I have the wood and you have the stone for making the fire. But where is the lamb for the sacrifice? Did you forget the lamb?"

"No, Isaac. God will show us a lamb, I'm sure."

They continued walking and finally reached the mountain. Isaac helped his father gather stones and together they built a small altar. Abraham put the wood on top of the altar and then turned to his son.

"Come here, Isaac."

Abraham began tying a rope around Isaac's arms and legs.

"Father, what are you doing?"

Huge tears flowed down Abraham's old face and into his mouth. The salt taste was bitter—

as if he had drunk from the sea.

"Isaac, my son—my only son. I...I love you. But God wishes you to be the sacrifice."

Abraham put Isaac on top of the wood and raised his knife to kill his son....

"Abraham! Abraham!" God called in a loud voice. "Do not harm the boy! I am now sure that you love me. You were willing to sacrifice your only son. I wanted to see if you would obey. And you did."

Abraham pulled Isaac from the altar and buried him in his arms. The tears flowed again, but now the salt was sweet in his mouth.

"Look there, father!" Isaac said.

Nearby was a ram caught by its horns in a bush. Abraham took the animal and he and Isaac sacrificed it together.

Then they returned to the servants and began the journey home.

Imagine how Sarah felt when she saw Abraham in the distance—and Isaac walking beside him!

And Abraham shouted:

"Sarah! It will be as God said. My family will be as numerous as the stars in the sky and as the grains of sand on the shore! Look! I bring you Isaac!"

25

The Twins

WHEN Isaac was forty years old, he married Rebekah. They had twin boys, called Esau and Jacob. Even before they were born the twins seemed to be fighting. Rebekah asked God about this, and God said:

"The twins will be fathers of two nations that will fight with each other. One nation will be stronger than the other. The older twin will be the servant of the younger twin."

And so it happened. Esau was born first and therefore had the right, when his father died, to most of his father's possessions. But Esau lost everything to Jacob. This is how it came about.

Esau was a strong, hairy man who liked to go out hunting. Jacob was quiet and liked to stay at home. One day Esau came home from a hunting trip and found Jacob making some soup.

"Let me have some of that soup," Esau said. "I'm tired out and hungry."

"Give me your right to father's possessions first," Jacob said.

"Father's possessions? What good are father's possessions to me now? I'm starved! I'm dying of hunger! Give me some soup."

"You must give me your promise first."

"All right. You have my promise."

Jacob gave Esau the soup. And so Esau, for a little soup, lost his right to his father's possessions.

Much later, when Isaac was old and dying, Esau might have gotten back his right to his father's possessions. But, again, he lost it. One day his father called him.

"Esau, my son!"

"Yes, father?"

"I am old now and blind. I don't know when I'll die. I want you to do something for me."

"Yes, father?"

"Take your bow and arrow and

bring me back some venison. Then cook it the way you know I like it and bring it to me. I will eat it and give you my blessing. And my blessing will give you the right to most of my possessions."

Esau left right away on the hunting trip. But Isaac's wife, Rebekah, heard what Isaac said to Esau. She called Jacob and told him about it. Then she said:

"Listen, Jacob, and do as I say. Go out to our herd and bring me two goats. I'll fix them the way your father likes. Then you can bring them to your father and he will bless you instead of Esau."

"But, mother, you know that Esau is hairy and my skin is smooth. If father touches me, he'll know I am not Esau. He'll know I'm trying to cheat him. Then he'll curse me instead of blessing me."

"I know all that, Jacob. Just do as I say! I'll take care of everything."

So Jacob went out and got the two goats for his mother. Rebekah prepared the meat the way Isaac liked it. Then she covered Jacob's smooth arms and neck with the hairy skins of the goats. She also took Esau's best clothes and made Jacob put them on.

"There!" she said. "Now bring the meat in to your father."

Jacob went to his father and said, "I'm back, father."

Issac, of course, could not see and he asked, "Who are you?"

"I am Esau," Jacob said, a little worried. "I did what you asked me to do. Come and eat the venison and then give me your blessing."

"But you found the venison so quickly," Isaac said.

"God showed me where to find it," Jacob answered, even more worried.

But Issac was suspicious. He said, "Come closer. I want to touch you. That way I'll know if you are really Esau."

Jacob cautiously moved closer to his father. His father touched him.

"How strange," he said. "Your voice sounds like Jacob's voice. But these feel like Esau's arms. Are you really Esau?"

"Yes, father," Jacob said.

"Strange.... Well, bring me the food. I will eat it."

When Isaac had finished eating, he still had doubts about whether it was Esau or Jacob who had brought him the meal.

"Come here," he said, "and kiss me."

When Jacob leaned over to kiss his father, Isaac smelled his clothes. They were Esau's clothes.

"Yes," he said, "these are Esau's clothes." And he gave Jacob his blessing: "May God give you the

riches of the earth. May nations serve you and bow down before you. Cursed will be he who curses you. Blessed will be he who blesses you."

Jacob left, and almost immediately Esau came running to his father.

"Father," he shouted, "come eat the venison I have brought and give me your blessing."

"And who are you?" Isaac asked, amazed.

"Why, I'm Esau! I brought you the venison you asked for."

Isaac began to tremble. "Who was it, then, that went hunting and brought me the venison?"

"Why, me, father—Esau. Now come and eat."

"No, no—I have already eaten. It must have been Jacob."

"What?"

"I have just finished eating the venison that Jacob brought me. I thought he was you. And I blessed *him*!"

Esau could not believe it. "Father," he cried, "bless me, too!"

"Your brother deceived me," Isaac said. "He already took your blessing."

"This is the second time!" Esau shouted. "First he took my rights as the oldest son—and now my blessing....Don't you have a blessing for me, father?"

"I have made Jacob your master, my son. I have given him my possessions. What is left for you, Esau?"

"But was that your only blessing, father? Give me a blessing, too!"

Isaac did not answer and Esau began crying. Finally, Isaac said, "You will live far from the riches of the world. You will live by the sword and you will serve your brother."

Heartbroken, Esau left his father. He hated Jacob for what he had done. And he thought to himself, "My father will die soon. Then I will kill Jacob."

Rebekah heard about Esau's plan. She told Jacob about it and advised him:

"Go away to my brother's place in Haran. Stay there until Esau cools off and forgets what you have done. Then I will send someone to bring you back."

Jacob did as his mother told him. And Esau and Jacob, the twins, did not meet again for a long time. When they did meet, Esau's anger had cooled off and the twins embraced and made up. But Jacob remained the stronger, as God had said.

Joseph's Coat

JACOB had twelve sons, but his favorite was Joseph. He even had a special coat made for him. The coat had many colors in it and it had long sleeves. The coat made Joseph look more important than his brothers and, of course, they were very unhappy about it. In fact, they disliked Joseph so much that they could hardly talk to him.

Another thing about Joseph that bothered them was that he was always telling them his dreams. For example, one day he said to them:

"Listen to this dream I had. I dreamt we were binding sheaves in the field and my sheaf stood up tall and your sheaves surrounded my sheaf and bowed to it."

"What does that mean?" his brothers asked angrily. "Do you mean you are going to be our king?"

Another day, Joseph told them:

"I had another dream. I think I saw the sun and the moon and eleven stars bowing to me."

This time his father heard the dream, and even he scolded Joseph.

"What kind of dream is that to have? I think I know what you are saying. I am the sun, your mother is the moon, and your brothers are the eleven stars. Does that mean, then, that we are all supposed to bow to you as if you were a king?"

Joseph's brothers stomped off in a rage and tried to forget the dream as soon as possible. But Jacob always remembered.

Some time later, Jacob said to Joseph, "Your brothers are tending the flock at Shechem. I am going to send you there."

"Fine, father," Joseph answered.

"Go and see how your brothers and the flock are doing. Then come and report to me."

So Joseph went off, dressed in his fine coat. When he got to Shechem, he could not find his brothers or the flock. Instead, he saw a man wandering around.

"What are you looking for?" the

man asked Joseph.

"I'm looking for my brothers. They were supposed to be here, tending the flock."

"Oh, they moved on. I heard them say they were going to Dothan."

And Dothan is where Joseph found them. But his brothers saw him coming and they said, "Oh-oh, here comes dream-boy."

"I suppose he wants us to bow down to him."

"Let's kill him instead."

"Yes, let's kill him and throw him down a well."

"We can tell father some wild animal ate him."

"Yes—then we'll see what kind of dreams he has!"

But one brother, Reuben, said:

"No. We cannot kill our own brother. Throw him into the well, if you like, but do not kill him." Reuben planned to come back later and save

Joseph. But, of course, he did not tell his brothers that.

So, when Joseph reached his brothers, they grabbed him, pulled his coat off, and threw him into a well that no longer had water in it. Then, quite calmly, they sat down to eat.

When they had finished eating they saw some merchants coming toward them. Their camels were loaded down with goods.

"They must be going to Egypt," Judah (one of the brothers) said. "Look, I have an idea. What good does it do us to let Joseph die in the well? Why don't we sell him to these merchants? He's our brother, after all, so let's not harm him."

The brothers agreed, and they sold Joseph to the merchants for twenty pieces of silver.

Now Reuben was not there when all this was going on. He returned later, and when his brothers were not looking, went to the well. He wanted to save Joseph. But when he looked over the edge, he saw that the well was empty. He ran to his brothers.

"The boy is gone!" he shouted. "What will I do now? What will I tell father?"

"Calm down, Reuben," his brothers told him. "We'll take care of it."

And they killed a goat and splattered the blood on Joseph's coat. Then they sent the coat to their father by messenger.

"Look at this coat your sons have found," the messenger told Jacob. "Isn't it Joseph's coat?"

Of course, there was no other coat like Joseph's, and his father recognized it immediately.

"It is my son's coat! Some wild animal has killed my son!" Jacob wailed in sorrow. He mourned his son for a long time, and no one could comfort him.

Joseph in Egypt

JOSEPH was sold by his brothers for twenty pieces of silver. The merchants who bought Joseph took him to Egypt and there they, in turn, sold him to a man named Potiphar.

Potiphar was an important official of Pharaoh, the Egyptian king. Joseph worked in Potiphar's house and God helped him, so that everything went well for Joseph. In fact, things went so well that Potiphar made Joseph his personal attendant and no one had more power in the house than Joseph, except Potiphar himself. So Joseph was happy in Egypt.

But, unfortunately, his happiness ended suddenly. One day Potiphar's wife falsely accused Joseph of trying to harm her when no one else was in the house. Potiphar was enraged and had Joseph thrown into jail.

But God helped Joseph, even in jail. Everyone liked Joseph, and in time he was put in charge of all the prisoners.

A while later, the man who prepared wine for Pharaoh displeased the king and was put in the same jail as Joseph. Naturally, since Joseph was in charge of all the prisoners, he came to know the wine preparer very well.

One day the wine preparer said to Joseph:

"I had a strange dream last night and no one seems to be able to make head or tail of it."

"Interpreting dreams is God's business," Joseph said. "I'm sure he will help me interpret it for you. Tell me your dream."

"Well—I saw a grapevine in front of me. It had three branches. And as soon as the branches budded, the buds became blossoms and then—right away—the blossoms became grapes. I had Pharaoh's cup in my hand. So I took the grapes and squeezed them and caught the juice in the cup. Then I put the cup in Pharaoh's hand."

"I can tell you what that means," Joseph said. "The three branches stand for three days. In three days Pharaoh will let you out of prison and give you back your old job. You will be Pharoah's wine preparer again."

"Now that *is* good news, isn't it! I hope you are right."

"I am right. But—when you are with the Pharaoh again, please ask him to let me out of this prison. I was falsely accused. There is no reason why I should be in jail."

"Why, certainly," the wine preparer promised.

Everything happened as Joseph said it would. Three days later, the wine preparer was let out of jail and got his old job back. But he was so happy about this that he forgot Joseph completely. And Joseph remained in jail for two more years.

Then it was Pharaoh's turn to have a dream. He dreamt he was standing near the Nile River, and coming toward him from the river were seven fat cows. They began to eat the grass near him. Then he saw seven other cows coming. But these were ugly and skinny. These cows went over to the fat cows and ate them all. Then Pharaoh woke up.

The next morning he sent for all the wise men of Egypt and asked them to tell him what the dream meant. But no one could do it. Pharaoh's wine preparer heard all this talk going on and he said to the king:

"Master, this dream reminds me of a promise I made and forgot about.

You remember when you were angry and put me in jail. Well, when I was there I had a dream and a young Hebrew called Joseph told me what it meant. And everything happened as he said it would. I think he could interpret your dream."

Pharaoh had Joseph brought to the palace immediately.

"My servant tells me you can interpret dreams," he said to Joseph.

"No, Pharaoh," Joseph said. "Interpreting dreams is God's business. But I am sure He will help me interpret your dream."

Pharaoh told Joseph the dream and Joseph said:

"God is telling you what He intends to do. The seven cows stand for seven years. You saw seven fat cows. That means there will be seven years when there will be plenty of food. But then you saw the seven skinny cows eat the fat cows. That means that the seven years of plenty will be followed by seven years of no food at all. This will happen very soon. You should name someone to control the food. He should put away enough food from the first seven years so that people will have something to eat during the next

seven. In that way your kingdom will not be destroyed."

Pharaoh nodded and said:

"You are a wise man, Joseph. Why should I look any further? Where in my kingdom will I find a man wiser than you? I will appoint you to take care of the food. Your power will be second only to mine. Whatever you say, all my people will do."

And Pharaoh took the ring from his own finger and put it on Joseph's. He also put rich clothes on Joseph and hung a gold chain around his neck.

"I name you governor of the kingdom of Egypt," he said. "You will ride in the finest chariot and no one in Egypt will move hand or foot unless you give permission."

Pharaoh also gave Joseph a new, much longer name. He called him Zaphenath-paneah.

Joseph set to work immediately. During the seven years of plenty he had food stored in warehouses until they could hold no more. Then the famine came, and for seven years there were no crops. Only Egypt had enough food. People came from all over the world to buy food from the Egyptians.

Joseph Saves His Family

FAMINE spread throughout the whole world. Even in the land of Canaan, where Joseph's family lived, there was no food. Jacob, Joseph's father, heard that there was food for sale in Egypt. He said to his sons:

"You stand around all day looking at one another. In the meantime we are starving. Why don't you go to Egypt and buy some food?"

So all of the brothers, except Benjamin, went to Egypt. Jacob did not let Benjamin go because he was the youngest and he did not want anything to happen to him.

Of course, since Joseph was in charge of all the food in Egypt, it was he who sold it. And so it happened that his brothers had to go to him for food. They did not recognize him, because he was dressed like an Egyptian, but he did recognize them. They bowed down before him, and Joseph remembered the dreams he had dreamed a long time ago.

"Where did you come from?" he said roughly, pretending to be angry.

"From Canaan," they answered. "We want to buy food."

"No—you are spies!" Joseph said. "You came here to see if Egypt is weak!"

"No, no, sir!" they said. "We came to buy food. We are brothers. We are honest people. Not spies!"

"I don't believe it! You want to hurt Egypt! You are spies!"

"No, sir, no. We are not spies. We are twelve brothers altogether. Our father is Jacob and we live in Canaan. Our father would not let Benjamin come because he is the youngest. One other brother, Joseph, is dead."

"You are spies, I say!" Joseph paused and then said, "All right. I'll give you a chance to prove you are telling the truth. One of you shall return to Canaan and bring Benjamin to me. The others will be kept in jail until he returns. If he does not come back with Benjamin, then I shall know you are spies."

Joseph kept his brothers in jail for

three days. Then he went to them.

"I will let all of you go, except one. You can take food back to Canaan so your families will not starve. But—mind you—bring back the youngest brother, or the brother left in jail will be killed."

The brothers began to talk among themselves.

"You know why this is happening? It is just what we did to Joseph! We paid no attention to him when he asked for mercy. We just threw him into the well and then sold him. Now there is no mercy for us."

Reuben said, "I told you not to harm the boy. But you wouldn't listen!"

They thought that Joseph did not understand what they were talking about. But he did. He left the room and began to cry. Later, he returned and made the soldiers put ropes around the brother named Simeon while the other brothers looked on.

"Now go and get the food!"

Joseph ordered his men to fill his brothers' sacks and, when they were not looking, to put their money back in the top of the sacks.

The brothers loaded the food and began the journey back to Canaan. At night they stopped and made camp. One of the brothers opened his sack to take out some food.

"What's this?" he said. "There's money in my sack."

All the brothers looked at each other, panic-stricken. "What is God doing to us? Now the Egyptians will think we are thieves. First spies—and now thieves!"

Thoroughly frightened, they broke camp and hurried on to Canaan. When they arrived they told their father, Jacob, all that had happened and how they had to take Benjamin back to Egypt. They opened all the sacks and found money in all of them. This made them even more afraid. Jacob was afraid, too, but he refused to let them take Benjamin.

"If anything happens to him," he said, "I will die from sorrow."

But the famine continued and the food they had brought from Egypt was soon gone. Jacob finally relented and let the brothers take Benjamin. They also took twice the amount of money they needed, so they could return the money found in the sacks.

In Egypt, the brothers went at once to Joseph. When he saw that Benjamin was with them, he said to his servant:

"Prepare me a meal. I will eat with these men in my house."

But the brothers were frightened. "He is sending us to his house to imprison us," they thought. "It is because of the money in our sacks."

So they said to the servant, "Sir, we were here before to buy food and later we found the money back in our sacks.

We don't know how it got there. But we have brought it back. Here!"

"Don't worry about it," the man said. "God must have put the money in your sacks. I remember being paid." Then he released Simeon from jail, and together all the brothers went to Joseph's house.

Joseph asked them if Jacob was alive and well. Then he began to seat them at the table. He began with the oldest and continued, in order, to the youngest. The brothers thought it strange that he could do this. How did he know in what order they were born? But they soon forgot it because they had a fine meal.

After the meal Joseph told his servant to fill his brothers' sacks with food and to put the money back as the last time.

"But," he added, "in Benjamin's sack put my silver cup."

The brothers left for Canaan. Then Joseph told his servant:

"Ride out after them. When you catch up with them ask them why they stole my cup."

The servant rode out after the brothers. They had not gone far and he soon reached them. He repeated what Joseph had said.

"What do you mean?" the brothers asked. "We didn't steal the cup. Why, we brought back the money we found in our sacks! Why would we steal his cup?"

"Very well," the servant said. "Let's look in your sacks. The one in whose sack the cup is found will be my master's slave. The rest of you may go free."

They dashed to the sacks. Of course, Benjamin found the cup in his sack. But they would not let Benjamin return alone. They all went back to the city and talked to Joseph.

"Sir, we do not know how this happened. But we have no excuse. We will all be your slaves rather than Benjamin alone."

Joseph shook his head. "No, I wouldn't think of doing such a thing. Benjamin will be my slave. The rest of you can return to your father."

Judah spoke up. "Sir, please listen. Do not be angry. Our father is old and he did not want to let Benjamin come

to Egypt because Benjamin is the youngest. But we persuaded him. Now, our father will die from sorrow if we do not bring Benjamin back. Please, let me stay in place of the boy."

Now Joseph could not stand the secrecy any longer. He told all his servants to leave the room. When he was alone with his brothers, Joseph began to cry. He cried so loudly that people outside could hear him. Through his tears, he said:

"I am Joseph. Is my father really still alive?"

The brothers could not answer him because they were so astounded at his loud crying.

Joseph finally controlled himself and said:

"Come closer. I am your brother, Joseph, whom you sold to the merchants. Do not feel sorry for me.

God wanted me here so that I could help you. Now, go—and bring Jacob, my father, and all your families. I will settle you all near me in Goshen, the richest land in Egypt."

The brothers returned to Canaan and told Jacob the news. And Jacob began the journey to Egypt.

When Joseph heard that his father was not far off, he ran out and jumped into his chariot and raced off to meet him. When he saw Jacob, he leaped out of the chariot and smothered his father in his arms. The two of them cried with happiness for a long time.

"I'm so happy I could die," Jacob said. "Now I have seen your face again—and I know you are alive and strong."

And Joseph settled his father and his brothers and their families in Goshen, and they lived there very happily for many years.

God Prepares a Leader

JOSEPH was a very powerful and very well-liked man in Egypt. He did so much good for the country that the Egyptians were willing to give him almost anything he wanted. So, when he brought his father and brothers and their families from Canaan and gave them one of the nicest places in Egypt to live in, no one objected. The Hebrews, as Joseph's people were called, were very happy in their new land. The families grew in numbers and the Hebrews became very powerful.

And so it was for many years. But then things changed. Joseph and his father and his brothers had all died by this time. The Pharaoh who had liked Joseph so much had also died, and there was a new king in Egypt. This new king did not remember all the good Joseph had done. He did not like the Hebrews—because he feared them. One day he said to his people:

"Look, we must do something about the Hebrews. They have become so numerous and strong that they are a danger to the country. If we ever had a war and they joined our enemies, we could never save ourselves."

"Right! The king is right!" everyone agreed.

"Now," the king continued, "I want to build two new cities. We will force the Hebrews to do all the heavy work. That way they'll be too tired to harm us. They won't become any more numerous."

So the Hebrews were forced to build the two cities of Pithom and Rameses. But the king was wrong. The Hebrews did increase, and they became still more powerful.

"We will make them slaves, then," the king said, "and give them the hardest work in Egypt. Let them make bricks. We must stop the Hebrews!"

But even this did not stop the Hebrews. They grew more and more numerous and powerful. Finally, the king gave this command:

"Let the Hebrew girls live—but

throw the boys into the river to drown."

It seemed as if God had forgotten the Hebrews completely. First, they had been made slaves, and now their children were being killed without mercy. But God had not forgotten. He was quietly preparing great things for the future.

At that time, a young Hebrew

couple had a baby boy. Since he was a boy, they hid him in the house because they did not want the Egyptians to kill him.

But babies cry when they are hungry and when they wake up and when they do not want to sleep. So it became too difficult to hide the baby any longer. The baby's mother made a basket and fixed it so that water could not get into it. It was like a little boat. She put the baby into the basket.

"Come with me," she said to her daughter. "I am going to put the baby in the river. You must stand close by to see what happens to him. Hide yourself in the grass."

So the baby's sister stayed near the river, hidden in the tall grass, and watched the basket bobbing gently on the water. In a short while she saw several young women coming towards the river. It was the princess and her maids! The king's own daughter!

The princess was preparing to bathe in the river when she noticed the basket floating along quietly.

"Bring me that basket," she told her maids.

The baby's sister was terrified. What would happen to the baby now? The maids brought the basket to the princess. She opened it and the baby began to cry.

"This must be a Hebrew baby," she said.

The baby's sister panicked. But

then she noticed that the princess was smiling. She decided to come out of her hiding place.

"Would you like me to find a Hebrew woman to take care of the baby for you?" she asked the princess. "Until he is older—then she will give him back to you."

"Yes—go and find a Hebrew woman," the princess said.

Of course, the girl ran directly to her own mother and brought her to the princess.

"Take this child," the princess said to the mother, "and take care of him until he is older. Then bring him back to me. I will pay you well. The Egyptians will not hurt him because I will treat him as my own son."

The mother happily did as she was told. When the boy was older, she took him back to the princess. The princess said:

"I will name him Moses because Moses means 'I took him out of the water.'"

And Moses grew up in the king's own palace. He was treated like a young prince.

When Moses was older he would often go to see the Hebrews, because they were his own people. Most of the Hebrews did not know this. They thought Moses was an Egyptian. But Moses knew, and he worried about the hard life his people had. One day he saw an Egyptian beating a Hebrew. Moses looked around to make sure no one was watching. Then he killed the Egyptian and hid the body in the sand.

The next day Moses was walking near the same spot, and this time he saw two Hebrews fighting with each other.

"Stop that!" he shouted. "Why should two countrymen fight?"

"And who do you think you are?" they answered. "Who made you judge over us? Are you going to kill us like you killed the Egyptian yesterday?"

Moses was struck dumb. "So everyone knows what I did," he thought to himself. "If the king hears of this, he'll have me killed!"

Moses knew it was now too dangerous for him to stay in Egypt, so he fled to the land of Midian. When he arrived there he found a well where many people came to get water. There were seven girls at the well, drawing out water for their sheep. Then some shepherds came and shouted:

"Out of here, girls! We don't have any time to wait for you. Go on! Out of here!"

Moses spoke up. "Wait a minute! Those girls were here first. You let them finish!"

The shepherds grumbled but, surprisingly, stepped back and let the girls finish.

The seven girls were sisters. When they got back home, their father called to them:

"How does it come you're back with the sheep so soon? Didn't the shepherds bother you today?"

"An Egyptian helped us," they said.

"And where is he?"

"Back at the well."

"Why did you leave him there? What were you thinking? Go back and invite him to supper!"

So Moses ate with the father and his daughters, and he liked the family so much he decided to stay with them. In fact, he later married one of the daughters. Her name was Zipporah.

Meanwhile, back in Egypt, the Hebrews were suffering more than ever. They cried to God for help. God listened to them and decided it was time to free these special people. He had prepared a leader for that purpose. But not even the man God had chosen to be leader knew that he had been prepared by God for such an important position.

He would know soon. The leader would be Moses!

The Reluctant Leader

OSES grew up in the king's palace in Egypt. But after he killed an Egyptian he had to flee to another country, called Midian. There he married Zipporah and took care of her father's sheep.

One day he led the sheep to the side of a mountain called Horeb or Sinai. A short distance in front of him he saw a bush on fire. The fire danced all through the bush, but the bush did not get any smaller.

"Now, isn't that strange," Moses said. "I'll have to take a closer look at this. I never saw a bush burning and not burning at the same time."

Moses moved closer. Suddenly he heard a strong voice come from the bush:

"Moses! Moses!"

"Ye—yes?" Moses could not see anyone.

"Don't come any closer."

Moses froze where he was.

"Take off your shoes," the voice said. "You are standing on holy ground."

Moses took off his shoes immediately.

"I am the God of your father," the voice continued. "I am the God of Isaac and Jacob."

Moses covered his eyes because he was afraid to look at God. Then God said:

"I see how my people, the Hebrews, are suffering in Egypt. I am going to free them. I will give them a new home in the land of Canaan. It will be a land of milk and honey. You will go to Pharaoh, the king, and tell him to let My people leave Egypt."

"But, who am I?" Moses said. "How could I go to Pharaoh and lead the Hebrews out of Egypt?"

"I will be with you," God answered. "And when you lead My people out of Egypt you will bring them here to this mountain to worship Me."

Moses scratched his head. "You want me to go to the Hebrews, then, and tell them that the God of their fathers sent me?"

"Yes."

"But suppose they ask me Your name. What will I tell them?"

"Tell them Yahweh sent you. Tell them that the God of Abraham, Isaac, and Jacob has sent you. Tell them that I have seen their suffering and I am going to help them. Then you will go with the oldest men to see Pharaoh."

"But . . . but," Moses still questioned, "suppose they don't believe me? Suppose they tell me God never appeared to me?"

"What is that you have in your hand?" God asked.

"Why—a stick I use as a cane."

"Throw it on the ground."

Moses threw the cane down and immediately jumped back. The cane had turned into a snake.

"Now, catch it by the tail," God said.

Gingerly, Moses moved toward the snake and grabbed it by the tail. The snake turned back into a cane.

"That will help them believe," God said. "Now—put your hand inside your shirt."

Moses did so, a little worried about what he might find there. When he took it out again, his hand was covered with leprosy.

"Put your hand back," God said.

And now, when Moses took his hand out, it was completely cured.

"There!" God said. "If they don't believe you, do those two signs for them. And if they don't believe the two signs, then take water from the river and pour it on the ground. The water will turn to blood. Then they will believe."

Moses thought about all of this for a few minutes. Then he said:

"Er...now...well, yes...but...but,

Lord, I've never been much of a talker. I...I can't make speeches. You know—I'm a slow speaker. I can't talk very well."

"Who made your mouth?" God asked, a bit annoyed. "Who is it that makes it possible for men to speak or not to speak?"

"Please—please!" Moses begged. "Please send someone else!"

Now God had had enough. He was angry with Moses. "Look!" God said. "There is your brother Aaron coming. No more excuses! I know he is a good speaker. You tell him what I've instructed you to do. He will do the speaking for you.... No—no! Not another word! Take your cane—and go!"

"But..."

"The king who wanted to kill you is dead—so don't try to make that excuse. No one will harm you. Go!"

Moses had no more excuses left. He went and met his brother, and when they had gathered their things they set out for Egypt: Moses, Aaron, and Moses' wife, Zipporah.

And the Hebrews believed Moses. They saw that God had sent him to be their leader.

A Stubborn King

IN SPITE of all his worries, Moses had little trouble in convincing the Hebrews that God had sent him to be their leader. They were willing to follow Moses out of Egypt. But then Moses had to talk to Pharaoh, the king. It was not so easy to convince Pharaoh.

Moses took Aaron with him because Aaron was to do all the talking. Together they entered the palace.

"Yahweh has sent us," Aaron said to Pharaoh. "Yahweh says: 'Let my people go. They will come to worship me in the desert.'"

"Who's Yahweh?" Pharaoh answered. "I don't know any Yahweh. So why should I listen to him? The Hebrews cannot go."

"But the God of the Hebrews has appeared to us. Let us make a three-day journey into the desert. Otherwise Yahweh will punish us."

"Look, you two," Pharaoh said, "what do you think you're doing? Stop trying to take the people from their work. Get back to your jobs! Out!"

Moses and Aaron left. Pharaoh called the chief slave driver.

"You have been giving the Hebrews straw to make bricks with. I want that stopped. Let them find their own straw."

"Yes, sir," the slave driver said.

"But, mind you, I want as many bricks as before. Make them work harder. That way they won't have time to listen to any fancy speeches from this Moses. They won't be asking to go out in the desert to worship Yahweh—whoever he is."

The slave driver told the Hebrews of Pharaoh's new order. The Hebrews ran all over the countryside looking for straw. This took time, of course, and they were not able to make as many bricks as before. But the slave drivers would hear no excuses. They whipped the Hebrews.

"You must make as many bricks as before!" they shouted. "It is the king's order! More bricks!"

Things became so bad that some of the Hebrew chiefs went to see Pharaoh.

"Sir, why are you treating us this way? We have to run back and forth to get the straw and that takes time. But the slave drivers demand more and more bricks."

"You are lazy, that's why!" the king said angrily. "You must have time on your hands. Otherwise you wouldn't be sending me that Moses with some story about Yahweh. You have time to go to the desert to worship Yahweh. So you have time to gather straw *and* make bricks. No! No straw! Back to work! And—I want more bricks. Do you hear? *More bricks*!"

The Hebrews went directly to Moses.

"Do you see what you have done?" they said to Moses. "May God punish you! Ever since you came with your stories, our life has been miserable. Let us alone. We don't want to be whipped any more."

Moses could not answer them. He knew they were right. Instead, he complained to God:

"Lord, why are you so hard on the Hebrews? Why did you send me here? Ever since I came, their lives are worse than before. You have done nothing for them."

"Pharaoh is stubborn," God said. "But you will see how I will punish him. I will force him to let the Hebrews go. I see how bad life is for the Hebrews now. But I will send them out of Egypt. I will give them a home in Canaan, the land of milk and honey. Go and tell the Hebrews that."

Moses did as he was told. But the Hebrews would not listen. They had heard enough of Moses' stories. Moses returned to Yahweh.

"Do you see how it is?" he asked.

"Never mind," God answered. "Go back to Pharaoh and tell him to let the Hebrews go."

"Look, Lord," Moses said, "even the Hebrews won't listen to me. What chance do I have with Pharaoh?"

"Take Aaron's cane with you. Do a marvel for Pharaoh."

Moses and Aaron went back to Pharaoh. But Pharaoh would not

listen. So Aaron took his cane and threw it on the floor before the king. The cane turned into a snake. Moses expected the king to be astounded, but all he said was:

"Very interesting. Very interesting, indeed." Then the king turned to his servant and said, "Send me my magicians!"

The magicians came bustling into the room.

"Magicians," the king said, "Moses here has been entertaining me with a trick. That snake you see on the floor was Moses' cane. Can you do anything like that?"

"Oh, yes, sir," the magicians said. They rummaged through their bags and pulled out canes. They threw the canes on the floor and their canes also turned into snakes.

Moses was worried. Pharaoh said, "So much for your trick, Moses...."

The king was about to continue, but then he noticed that Moses' snake had eaten all the others!

Moses looked at Pharaoh, expecting him to now change his mind and let the Hebrews go. But Pharaoh only said:

"Out!"

Pharaoh was a stubborn man. But he did not know how strong Yahweh was.

He would know soon.

Plagues

GOD had decided to free the Hebrews. But Pharaoh would have no part in God's decision. He did not believe in God. So God had to convince Pharaoh. He sent Moses and Aaron to perform wonders—to bring plagues on the land of Egypt.

God first had Moses turn the water of Egypt into blood, so that no one could drink it. Then God sent frogs to cover the whole country. But Pharaoh's magicians could do the same things, and Pharaoh would not change his mind. Then God said to Moses:

"Tell Aaron to hit the dust on the ground with his cane. The dust will turn to lice."

Moses did as he was told. This time Pharaoh's magicians could not do the same thing.

"This must be God's work," they said. "We have no power to do such a thing."

But Pharaoh would not listen to them. "Get out of my sight!" he said.

"You're no help to me at all!"

God was not finished yet. "Tell Pharaoh," God said to Moses, "that I will send flies to cover Egypt tomorrow if he will not let My people go. They will bother the Egyptians—but not the Hebrews."

Moses told Pharaoh what God had said but, again, Pharaoh would not listen. So, the next day, swarms of flies covered Egypt. They were in the air and crawling on the ground. They even filled the houses of the Egyptians.

Pharaoh sent for Moses and Aaron.

"All right!" he said to them. "I have had enough. Go sacrifice to your God—but do it here in Egypt."

"But you know we can't do that," Moses said. "The Egyptians do not like our sacrifices. They worship the

animals we use for our sacrifices. If we make a sacrifice in Egypt, the Egyptians would attack us. We must leave the country."

"Very well. If you must. But don't go far. And get rid of these flies!"

"They will be gone tomorrow."

And it happened as Moses said. The next day the flies had disappeared. But when Pharaoh saw that the flies had gone, he changed his mind and sent word to Moses that the Hebrews could not leave the country.

God said to Moses, "Go again and tell Pharaoh to let the Hebrews go. If he refuses, I will send disease on the animals of Egypt. The cattle will die."

Of course, Pharaoh would not listen. The cattle became sick and died, but Pharaoh would not change his mind. Then God let boils appear on all the Egyptians—but still the king remained stubborn.

God sent Moses to Pharaoh again.

"You still refuse to let the people go," Moses said to Pharaoh. "Therefore tomorrow, about this time, God will send hail that will destroy the land."

"Get out of my sight!" Pharaoh shouted.

The next day Moses stretched his hand toward the sky. Immediately thunder rumbled and shook the earth. Hail fell in sheets. It blasted strong trees to pieces, knocked down men and animals alike, and pounded them until they were dead.

Pharaoh sent for Moses immediately. "Stop the hail, Moses—and this horrible roar of thunder! I admit I was wrong. I admit it! Please—do something. I promise I'll let your people go. Please!"

"I know your promises. Yes, I'll ask God to stop the hail. But I know you. As soon as you feel safe, you'll change your mind again."

And so it happened. The hail stopped—and Pharaoh changed his mind!

God spoke to Moses: "Go to Pharaoh again."

"But what is the use?" Moses argued. "It will be the same thing all over again. Who can talk to that stubborn man?"

"Do not worry. I have let Pharaoh be stubborn on purpose. Now the Hebrews can see how much I love them. They have not been harmed by any of the plagues. They can tell their children and grandchildren for ages to come about all the wonders God did for them when they were in Egypt. Now—go to Pharaoh again."

As Moses and Aaron entered the room, Pharaoh said, "You again? Is there no end to this?"

"It is your own fault," Moses told him. "You will not let the Hebrews go. Now God will send locusts to devour what is left of your ruined country."

"I do not fear your God. Leave me alone."

As Moses and Aaron were leaving, the Pharaoh's advisers said to the king:

"Sir, how long is this going to go on? Let the Hebrews go. Don't you see that Egypt is almost destroyed?"

"Do you think I am blind?" Pharaoh called Moses and Aaron back. "Whom do you want to take to the desert?" he asked.

"Why—all of us, old men, young men, women, and children."

"Oh, no, you don't! Not everyone! The old men can go, that's all. No one else. That is my last word on the subject."

Moses and Aaron did not answer.

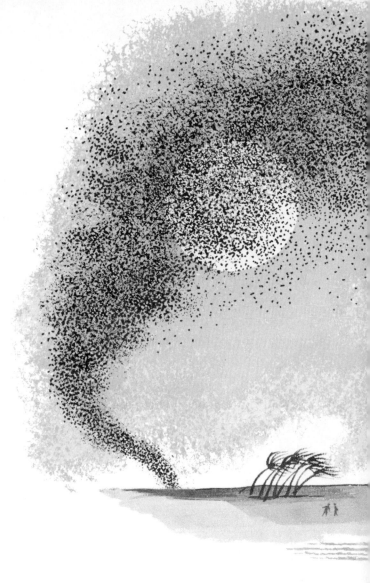

They turned and left the palace.

The next day Moses stretched his cane over Egypt. The wind changed its direction. It blew from the east all that day and night. The next morning Moses could see what looked like a black cloud coming from the direction of the sun. It was a great mass of locusts. Faster and faster it came. The sky grew almost black. Moses could

hear the *swish-swish* of the locusts' wings grow louder and louder. And then the locusts were everywhere, in the trees, on the ground, and in the air. They ate everything in sight. Whatever the hail had not destroyed, the locusts chewed until the land was bare.

Pharaoh sent for Moses. "I am sorry. I have sinned. Please—just once more. Take the locusts away and I will let the people go."

So Moses talked to God and God changed the direction of the wind and all the locusts flew off. And what did Pharaoh do? Again, he refused to let the Hebrews go.

"We are not finished yet," God said to Moses. "Stretch your hand toward the sky and darkness will come over Egypt."

Moses did as he was told, and for three days Egypt was as dark as midnight. No one could see or move.

Pharaoh called Moses. "Go and offer your sacrifice! But don't bring any animals."

"No," Moses answered, "we must take our animals."

"Agh! No! No! No! Get out of my sight! I'm sick of seeing your face!"

Moses left. God spoke to him again:

"The time has come. I will work one more wonder. Pharaoh will not be able to resist any longer. He will let my people go!"

The Hebrews would soon be free!

59

Exodus

You have refused to let the Hebrews go again and again," Moses said to Pharaoh.

"I won't listen!" Pharoah answered.

"Yes, you will! Tonight, at midnight, God will pass through Egypt and the oldest son of every family will die."

"I won't listen, I tell you!"

"Your oldest son will die, too! Can't you see the harm you are bringing to your country?"

"Don't try to teach me about my country. I'm not listening!"

"You will hear crying all over Egypt. Do you want that?"

"I can't hear a word you're saying."

Moses grew angry. "Well, I'll shout it so you can hear! There will be so much sadness tonight in Egypt that you will come and beg us to leave. Do you hear? Beg us!"

Moses, red-faced with anger, turned and left. He went to the Hebrews and told them the instructions God had given him:

"Prepare yourselves for the journey. God will now lead us to the promised land, the land of milk and honey. You must be ready to move at a moment's notice. But, first, take a sheep or a goat and kill it and sprinkle its blood on your doors. Then stay inside your houses. When God passes through Egypt tonight, He will see the blood and not harm your oldest sons. We will celebrate this night every year. We will call the feast 'Passover' because God passed over our houses and did not harm our children. Now, hurry! Do as you are told!"

The Hebrews hurried to prepare for the journey. And that night, at midnight, God passed through Egypt and the oldest son in every Egyptian family died. Even Pharoah's own son died. And all over Egypt you could hear people crying.

Pharaoh sent for Moses and Aaron in the middle of the night. "Leave Egypt!" he said. "Take the Hebrews away from my people."

Moses and Aaron hurried to tell the Hebrews. All along the way Egyptians shouted to them:

"Hurry!"

"Get out of Egypt tonight!"

"We'll all be dead if you don't hurry!"

The Hebrews gathered together and began the march. There were 600,000 men alone in the crowd, not counting women and children. And it was God Himself who showed them the way. A pillar of cloud led

the way during the day and, at night, a pillar of fire.

When the Hebrews had left, the Egyptians began to have doubts. Should they have let the Hebrews go? Some advisers went to Pharaoh.

"What have we done, Sir?" they said.

"We should not have let all the Hebrew slaves go."

"Who will do the work now?"

Pharaoh answered, "Yes, we have made a mistake. We should never have let them go. Get my army ready! We will bring the Hebrews back!"

The Egyptian army, mounted on glittering chariots, with Pharaoh at their head, roared out of the city.

The Hebrews had reached the Red Sea by this time. They had made a camp there. Some people at the back of the crowd noticed the Egyptians coming in the distance. Word spread through the crowd:

"The Egyptians!"

"Pharaoh's army!"

The shouts grew louder and louder until they reached Moses.

"Why have you done this to us, Moses?"

"Why should we die here in the desert? Weren't there enough graves in Egypt?"

"You're nothing but trouble, Moses!"

"We'd rather work in Egypt!"

"Better to live in Egypt than to die here!"

Moses shouted back at them, "Quiet! Don't fear! God will take care of us! Calm down!" Then Moses spoke to God: "Lord, look at what has happened now. Are we all to die here?"

"Moses," God answered, "I wish you would stop your whining. March on! Raise your cane and stretch your hand over the sea."

Moses obeyed and startled shouts came from the crowd.

"The water!"

"Look at the water!"

The sea was parting before them. There was a dry path from one side of the sea to the other, with walls of water on either side.

"March!" shouted Moses, and the Hebrews began walking through the sea, laughing and singing.

Pharaoh, from the distance, could see that the Hebrews were escaping.

"Faster!" he shouted to his army. "On them like lightning! Let no one escape!"

The Egyptian army thundered toward the sea. Down into the dry path of the sea they went, and the noise of their chariots clattered off the walls of water. Through the sea they marched until they were almost upon the Hebrews. Then God confused them. The wheels of their chariots stuck, horses stumbled, and men flipped over their wagons. The army sprawled every-which-way. Some chariots went in circles, others broke down completely.

"Retreat!" the Egyptians began to shout.

"Retreat! Their God is fighting for them!"

The Egyptians turned and rolled as fast as they could back to the sea.

When the entire army was in the dry path leading through the sea, God spoke to Moses:

"Now! Hold up your cane!"

Moses did so. All at once the water walls caved in. Water gushed on top of the Egyptians. The whole army was caught. Chariots screeched. Horses snorted. Men screamed. Then quiet fell over the whole sea. Soon, empty chariots bobbed to the surface of the water. The Egyptian army was drowned!

The Hebrews were free at last!

It would take the Hebrews forty years to reach the land of milk and honey. There would be much suffering before they got there. But God would always help them. For now—the Egyptians were defeated.

God's people were free!

Samson

SAMSON was one of the leaders of Israel. He was exceptionally strong. The secret of his strength was a promise that his parents made for him before he was born. Samson would never cut his hair, never take strong drink, nor eat anything that was not specially prepared. Because of this promise, God gave Samson great strength.

At that time the Hebrews were living in Israel. But their enemies, the Philistines, controlled the country. The Philistines had great fear of Samson because of his strength. They had tried to arrest him several times, but each time he easily escaped from them.

Then Samson went to a place called Sorek. He fell in love with a girl there. Her name was Delilah. When the Philistines heard that Samson had fallen in love, they sent for the girl.

"Samson has a secret for his strength," they said to Delilah.

"I don't know his secret," Delilah answered the Philistines.

"But he loves you and if you ask him, he'll tell you. Once we know the secret, we can capture him."

"Oh, I couldn't do that," Delilah said.

"Look," they said, "there are five of us here. Each one of us will give you a thousand dollars if you find out his secret. That's five thousand dollars!"

Delilah thought for a moment. She had never heard of so much money. Then she said, "All right. I'll do it."

Later that day when she was with Samson, Delilah said, "Where do you get all your strength, dear? What's your secret?"

"Why do you want to know?" Samson said.

"Oh—no reason, darling. I'd just like to know."

"Hmmm. Well—if I were tied with leather strings, I'd be as weak as anyone."

"My! How interesting!"

Delilah then went to the Philistines and told them what Samson had said.

They gave her the leather strings and returned with her to the house. The Philistines stayed in the next room while Delilah waited for Samson to fall asleep. Then she tied up Samson with the leather strings. When she had finished, she screamed:

"Samson! The Philistines are here!"

Samson jumped up from the bed and snapped the strings as if they were made of eggshells. The Philistines scrambled out of the house.

"Ha, ha, ha!" Samson roared at them.

"You're not only laughing at them, Samson," Delilah said. "You're laughing at me, too. Why did you lie to me, sweetheart?"

"Oh, don't be silly," Samson said.

"Please—please tell me the truth. What is the secret of your strength?"

"Well—" Samson said with a little grin, "if you got ropes that had never been used before and tied me up tightly, then I'd lose all my strength."

Delilah went back to the Philistines.

"Are you sure he told you the secret this time?" they said to Delilah. "That was a close call before. Five thousand dollars is five thousand dollars, after all. We want the truth for our money."

"Yes, I'm sure," Delilah said.

"All right. Here's the new rope."

They returned to the house. Again, the Philistines waited in the next room. When Samson was asleep,

Delilah tied him with the new rope. Then she shouted:

"Samson! It's the Philistines again!"

Samson jumped up and broke the rope as if it were thread. The Philistines banged into each other trying to get out the door.

"Samson!" Delilah cried. "Oh, Samson, my love, you're treating me like a little fool. Why do you tell me lies? Tell me the true secret of your strength."

"You really are curious, aren't you?"

"Oh, Samson . . . ," Delilah whimpered.

"Well—I'll tell you. It's a little complicated. You see your loom there—that thing you make cloth on?"

"Yes."

"Well, if you take my hair and put it into the loom, the way you do with thread, and weave my hair—you know, make cloth from my hair—why, then I'd have no strength at all."

Delilah ran to the Philistines.

"That's crazy!" they said. "That's the stupidest thing we ever heard—make cloth from his hair! We pay you good money and you come with stories like that?"

"But it's true!" Delilah insisted. "That's what he told me. And he was serious."

"Well—"

"It's true, I tell you!"

"All right. Let's try it."

When Samson was asleep, Delilah pulled the heavy loom close to his head and began making cloth from his hair. Samson's hair was very long, so it took her a while. When she had finished, she shouted:

"Samson! The Philistines!"

Samson jumped up, pulled his hair loose, and broke the loom as if it were made of toothpicks. The Philistines were halfway down the street before he finished.

"Oh, Samson!" Delilah screamed in a rage and stamped her foot. "You don't love me! You can't love me! You're a liar! Liar! Liar!"

And for days she kept after Samson, whining, shouting, crying, begging, pouting.

Finally, Samson said, "I can't stand it any more. I'll go out of my mind with the noise you make. I'll tell you the secret."

"Honest?"

"Yes, honest. Just keep quiet, will you?"

"Yes, dear." Delilah was all smiles.

"My hair has never been cut in all my life. My parents made a promise to God before I was born. If my hair is cut, I will lose all my strength."

"Oh, darling—I know you're telling the truth now."

"Just keep quiet—*please*!"

Delilah told the Philistines:

"Come—just once more! I am sure he has told me the truth this time."

So while Samson slept they cut off his hair and Delilah screamed again:

"Samson! The Philistines!"

Samson jumped up in bed ready to run after the Philistines. But then he felt his head and he knew that he had lost his strength. The Philistines seized him and bound him. They blinded him and threw him into prison.

Later, the Philistines had a great feast to celebrate Samson's capture. They made a huge sacrifice to their god, Dagon. And they drank and shouted and danced in the enormous temple that they had built to Dagon.

"Send Samson out," they shouted, "so we can have some fun with him."

"Send us Samson!"

"Samson! Samson! Samson!"

So Samson was brought out of prison. The people did not realize that his hair had been growing back.

"There he is!" they laughed.

"Samson, the weakling!"

Samson was blind. He said to the boy who was leading him by the hand:

"Lead me to the two pillars that hold up the temple. I want to lean on them."

The boy led him toward the pillars. The temple was jammed with Philistines. There were even many people on the roof. And they all clapped and laughed as they saw the boy leading Samson through the temple.

Samson prayed quietly, "My God, give me back my strength—just this once."

The boy finally reached the pillars. Samson put one hand on each of them.

"I will die!" he shouted. "But all of you will die with me!"

With all his strength he pushed the pillars. They smashed in pieces and the whole temple came crashing down to the floor. Samson died in the rubble, but he had also destroyed many Philistines.

His brothers came later and took Samson's body back home and buried it beside that of his father.

And the Hebrews mourned the strongest man they had ever known.

Samuel

HANNAH was a good Israelite woman. But she had no children and that made her very sad. It made her so sad that she often could not eat. Her husband, Elkanah, tried to console her.

"Hannah, why do you cry so much? Look—you're not eating again. That is not good for you. Isn't having me better than having ten sons?"

But nothing Elkanah said could make Hannah feel better. One day she decided to go the Temple to pray. She wanted to pray out loud to God, but she was so sad that she could only mumble.

A priest named Eli, who was also the leader of Israel, was standing close by. Hannah did not see him. Since she was mumbling, Eli could not make out what she was saying.

"Here, woman!" he said. "How long are you going to stand there mumbling like that?"

Hannah turned to Eli, surprised.

"Oh!" she said. "I didn't see you there. I was praying."

"A strange way to pray! What were you praying for?"

"I have no children," Hannah answered. "I was begging God to send me a child. I told God that if He gives me a son, I will let him serve God all his life."

"Go home in peace," Eli said. "And may God grant you a son."

Hannah went home feeling much happier. And, sure enough, within a year she had a son. She called him Samuel. She loved Samuel dearly, but she also remembered the promise she had made to God. So, when Samuel was old enough, she took him to the Temple. Eli, the priest, took care of Samuel and Samuel grew strong and served God in the Temple.

Eli also had two sons, Hophni and Phinehas. They were priests, too, but very bad priests. They were greedy and unkind.

The people who loved God would

bring animals to sacrifice to God. When the meat was cooking, Hophni and Phinehas would send their servant with an enormous fork that had three prongs. The servant would plunge the fork into the pot, and anything that came up on the fork he took to the priests.

And the people would say, "That's too much! God says that priests can have their fair portion. But these priests are taking nearly everything! They are too greedy!"

But the servant would pay no attention. He would just plunge the fork into the pot and take the meat back to the priests.

And then the priests became fussier yet. They did not want boiled meat anymore, but raw meat, so they could roast it themselves.

The people said, "What is this now? Where will these priests stop? If they take the meat raw, then we can't even make the sacrifice the way God wants us to. Tell the priests to wait."

"No!" the servant answered. "Give me the meat raw—or I'll take it by force!"

Hophni and Phinehas did many other evil things, also. Of course, everyone was complaining about them. Eli, their father, scolded them.

"Why do you do these things?

You make yourselves fat on religion. You are sinning against God Himself."

"Don't bother us, father," they said. "We'll do as we please. Who cares about the people?" And they continued acting in their greedy way. From then on Eli just ignored what they were doing. He did not try to correct them.

Then one night, when Samuel was asleep in the Temple, he heard a voice calling:

"Samuel! Samuel!"

"Yes?" Samuel wiped his eyes, got up, and ran to Eli.

"You called me?" he said to Eli.

"Wha—Sam—" Eli mumbled, still half asleep. "No, I didn't call you. Go back to bed." Eli turned over and began to snore. Samuel shrugged his shoulders, yawned, and went back to his bed. He was just drifting off to sleep when he heard the voice again:

"Samuel! Samuel!"

Samuel sat up in bed and looked around. "What's wrong with Eli?" he thought. "He tells me to go back to bed, then he calls me again."

He went back to Eli.

"Eli?"

"Eh?" Eli snorted, trying to wake up. "Oh—it's you again, Samuel?"

"I heard you call."

"No—no—I didn't call. Go back to b..." Eli was asleep before he finished talking.

Samuel shook his head. "Poor Eli," he said, and went back to bed. But this time he did not sleep. And he heard the voice again:

"Samuel! Samuel!"

He ran immediately to Eli. But Eli was still snoring.

"Eli, Eli—wake up!"

"Eh?" Oh . . . Sam . . ."

"No, Eli—wake up. I know you called."

Eli struggled up to a sitting position. "What are you talking about? What has gotten into you, my son? Are you going to spend the whole night waking me up?"

"But I heard you call."

"I didn't call, I tell you. It wasn't me. It wasn't.... Are you sure you heard a call?"

"Yes, I'm positive."

"Hmm...strange. Do you know what I think, Samuel? I think it must be God calling you. Now, go back to bed. And if you hear the voice again you must say, 'Yes, Lord, speak—your servant is listening.' Can you remember that?"

"Yes," Samuel answered and went back to bed.

The voice called again.

Samuel answered, "Yes, Lord, speak—your servant is listening."

"Samuel," God said, "I am about to do a terrible thing in Israel. I am going to destroy the family of Eli because his sons live such evil lives. I will destroy Eli, too, because he did not make his sons change their lives. They will all be destroyed."

Samuel lay still in his bed until morning thinking about what God had said. He knew Eli would be curious, but he did not want to tell him such a terrible thing. In the morning, Eli called him.

"Did God speak to you, Samuel?"

"Oh...er..."

"Don't hold back, Samuel. What did God say?"

"But..."

"Samuel!"

"God said...said He would...

destroy your family because your family... because your family is bad."

Eli bowed his head. "He is God. He will do what He thinks is right."

But nothing happened. Eli grew fat and old and blind, and his sons were as wicked as ever. Samuel grew to be a fine young man. He often wondered about the words that God had spoken. Everything seemed to be the same as before. Perhaps he had not understood what God had said.

But then Israel had a battle with their neighbors, the Philistines. The men of Israel knew how powerful the Philistines were, so they asked Eli if they could bring the Ark with them to the battlefield. The Ark was the most sacred thing that Israel had. Years before, after Moses had received the tablets of the ten commandments from God, God had told him to build an Ark and to put the tablets in it. And wherever the Ark went, God went with it.

Eli was worried about letting the Ark go to the battlefield. But the men insisted, and he let them take it. He sent Hophni and Phinehas along to take care of the Ark.

When the army of Israel had left, Eli sat on a high stool near the entrance to the town, waiting for

someone to come with news of the battle. He waited many days.

Then one day a man came running down the road toward the town. His clothes were torn and he was injured. He was screaming at the top of his voice.

Eli called out, "What is all this screaming about?"

The man ran to Eli. "I just came from the battlefield," he said.

"What has happened?" Eli asked.

"We were defeated! We have lost to the Philistines!"

"And my sons? How are my sons?"

"They are dead!"

Eli was almost too afraid to ask the next question: "And the Ark?"

"The Ark has been captured! We are ruined!"

When Eli heard about the Ark he was so shaken that he fell back off his high stool. He broke his neck and died immediately. God had done what He had told Samuel He would do. Eli and his sons were all dead.

The people then took Samuel as their priest and leader. And the Philistines were soon forced to return the Ark to Israel.

Samuel was a good priest. He dedicated all of his life, as his mother had promised, to the service of God.

Saul

SAMUEL was a good leader of Israel for many years. But as he grew older the work became too difficult for him. So Samuel retired and named his oldest sons, Joel and Abiah, as leaders in his place. But his sons were not at all like Samuel. They were too interested in money. Very soon the people of Israel were fed up with them. They came to Samuel and said:

"Look—you are too old to be leader, and your sons are thieves. We want a king like other countries have."

"Israel has never had a king!" Samuel said. "God is our king!"

"No! We need a king," the people insisted.

Samuel was quite unhappy. He spoke to God:

"The people want a king, Lord. I think that is disgraceful! You are our king."

"Do as they say, Samuel, and do not worry," God said. "After all, they are rejecting Me—not you. They have never been content. Give them a king. But tell them what having a king will be like."

Samuel returned to the people and said, "Do you know what having a king will be like?"

"Of course we do!" they answered.

"Are you sure?"

"Yes! Yes!"

"Do you know that your sons will have to serve in the king's army? Do you know they will have to work like slaves for him? Do you know that your daughters will be taken to be cooks and maids for the king? Do you know? Answer me!"

The crowd was quiet. A few murmured, "Yes."

"Do you know the king will take your best fields! Your best grapes and olives will be his. Do you know the king will tax you? Answer me!"

The crowd was silent. Many looked down at the ground and shuffled their feet.

"A day will come when you will cry like babies because of your king! But don't expect God to listen to you

76

then!"

The people stood there, stunned. But, slowly, people here and there in the crowd began to murmur.

"Who cares?"

"A king would still be better than Samuel's sons."

"Don't listen to Samuel."

And the murmuring grew louder until everyone was shouting:

"No! We want a king!"

"Give us a king!"

"He will lead us in war!"

"We will be a strong nation!"

"A king! A king! A king!"

Samuel let them shout. Then he said, "All right! You can have your king! Go home, all of you!"

And a roar broke from the crowd: "HURRAH!" Then the crowd began to break up and the people, shouting and singing, went home.

Not far from the place where the crowd asked Samuel for a king, there lived a man named Kish. He had a son who was said to be the handsomest man in Israel. He stood head and shoulders taller than anyone in the country. His name was Saul.

Saul worked for his father, taking care of the cattle. One day some of his father's donkeys strayed off, and Kish said to Saul:

"Saul, my son, take one of the servants and go and look for the donkeys."

So Saul and the servant went. They traveled for three days, but they could not find the donkeys. Finally Saul said to the servant:

"Come on—let's go home. Father will have stopped worrying about the donkeys by now and will be worrying about us."

"No, wait," the servant said. "See that town over there? I hear there is a man of God there. He's called Samuel. They say everything he says comes true. Maybe he can tell us where the donkeys are."

"Good idea! Come!"

As they came near the town, they saw some girls at a well.

"Do you know where Samuel is?" Saul asked.

"Yes. He's in town. He just arrived. There is to be a big feast today. You will see him as soon as you get into town."

Now, the day before, God had spoken to Samuel and said, "Tomorrow, at about this hour, a man will come to you. You will make him king of Israel." When Saul came toward Samuel, God spoke again: "That is the man."

"Do you know where Samuel is?" Saul asked, as he came near.

"I am Samuel. Come to the feast. Tomorrow I will tell you everything you want to know. As for the donkeys—they have already been found."

Saul was astounded that Samuel should know about the donkeys.

"Besides," Samuel continued, "there is no reason for you to worry about donkeys. All the riches of Israel will be yours."

"But..." Saul answered, "but I am a humble man from a humble family. Why do you say such a thing to me?"

Samuel did not answer but led Saul to the feast. He made Saul sit at the head of the table. Saul looked around at all the other people at the table—about thirty altogether. "What's happening?" he thought to himself. He looked at the servant, but the servant only shrugged his shoulders. Then the best part of the meal was served to Saul. He ate because he was hungry from his trip, but he hardly tasted the food. Everything was so strange!

That night Saul and the servant slept on the roof of one of the houses. In the morning, Samuel called to them from the street:

"Get up. I am leaving."

Saul and the servant climbed down to the street.

"Go on ahead," Samuel said to the servant. Then he took a jar of oil, poured it on Saul's head, and kissed him. "God has anointed you! You are now the king of Israel!"

Saul could only stand there—with his mouth open.

"I will give you proof that what I say is true," Samuel continued. "When you leave me you will meet two men. They will say, 'The donkeys have been found. Your father is now worried about you.' Then, as you travel further, you will meet three men, one carrying three goats, another carrying three loaves of bread, and the third carrying a skin of

wine. They will give you two loaves of bread. Later, you will meet some prophets. They will be led by people playing harps, tambourines, flutes, and lyres. The spirit of God will then come upon you and you will feel like a new man. By these signs, you will know that what I say is true. Then, go home, and wait for more instructions from me."

Samuel left. Saul still could not talk. But everything happened as Samuel said it would. And Saul knew that God had chosen him to be king of Israel. When he got home, Saul told his father what had happened, but he did not mention that Samuel had made him king.

Soon after that, Samuel called all the people to a place called Mizpah. Here Samuel cast lots to choose the king of Israel and, because it was God's will, the lot fell to Saul, the son of Kish.

"Where is Saul?" the people asked.

They looked all around but could not find Saul. Saul was afraid because he knew that he was God's choice to be king. He had hidden himself among the baggage the people had brought on the trip.

Finally, God said to the people, "He is hidden among the baggage."

The people ran and brought Saul out. Then they formed a large circle, and put him in the middle. Saul stood tall—to his full height, and the people had to look up to him.

Then Samuel shouted, "Do you see the man God has chosen to be your king? There is no one like him in all of Israel!"

And the people cheered:
"Long live the king!"

God Prepares a New King

IN THE beginning Saul was a fine king. But little by little he began to change. As happens so often, power went to his head. He began to refuse to obey God, and because of this God turned against Saul.

The servants in the palace noticed a change in the king. He was moody all day and, worse yet, he was afraid of everything. Now, Saul was a giant of a man, head and shoulders taller than anyone in Israel. What a sad thing it was to see such a man afraid of his own shadow!

The servants talked among themselves:

"We must do something to soothe the king."

"Yes, he cannot go on this way."

"I have an idea. I know a young man who plays the harp very well. We should ask the king to bring him here."

"And the next time the king is in one of his bad moods, the young man can play the harp! That's a splendid idea! We'll ask the king the next chance we get."

About that same time, God was speaking to Samuel:

"I regret having made Saul king. He refuses to obey me. It is time to prepare for a new king."

"But, Lord," Samuel said, "if I do that, Saul will surely kill me."

"I will tell you what to do," God said. "Saul will not know. Take a calf and go to Bethlehem. There you will meet a man named Jesse. Tell him you have come to offer sacrifice. Then when you have offered the sacrifice, ask Jesse to bring his sons to you."

Samuel did as he was told. He sacrificed the calf in Bethlehem, and when he was finished he said to Jesse:

"Bring your sons to me."

Jesse brought Eliab first.

Eliab was a fine-looking man, and when Samuel saw him he thought, "This must be the one." But God said to Samuel:

"Do not pay any attention to what

the man looks like. I do not see as man sees. I look into the heart. This is not the one."

Samuel told Jesse that he wanted to see his other sons. Jesse brought nine more sons, but Samuel rejected them all one by one. Then he said, "Are these all of your sons?"

"There is one more," Jesse answered. "David. He is taking care of the sheep out on the hill. Probably playing his harp, too."

"Send for him," Samuel said.

When David came into sight, God said to Samuel:

"This is the one. Anoint him."

So, in front of the family, Samuel took oil and poured it on David's head. The spirit of God came upon David. But Samuel said no more.

In Saul's palace, the servants finally

found a chance to talk with the king.

"Lord Saul," they said, "you should have a harpist to play for you when you are feeling bad."

"Yes. I think that might help. Do you know anyone who plays the harp?"

"There is a young man in Bethlehem who plays quite well. His name is David."

"Send for him!"

And so it was that David entered the palace of the king. Saul liked him. And David played the harp for Saul to soothe him when he felt bad.

Time would pass before David became king. But everything was now prepared: God had chosen David, Samuel had anointed him, and David was living in the palace.

David would be king. But much would happen before that.

David and Goliath

THE Philistines were one of the strongest enemies that Israel had. They had often fought with Israel and, more often than not, the Philistines had won.

Now the Philistines were preparing for war again. They brought their troops together at Shochoh. There they took possession of a hill. Saul, the king of Israel, also brought his army to that place and lined it up on a hill across from the Philistines. The two armies thus stood facing each other on the two hills with a small valley stretching between them.

One of the Philistine soldiers marched down the hill toward the army of Israel. The men of Israel shuddered when they saw him. He was over nine feet tall! His armor alone was heavier than any man in the army of Israel. On his head was a huge bronze helmet, and his shield was large enough to be a wagon wheel. His name was Goliath.

When he spoke it sounded like the roar of a lion, and the roar echoed back and forth across the valley.

"Israel! Why stand you there? I am a Philistine! You are slaves of Saul!"

It seemed as though the hills themselves shook with the sound of Goliath's voice.

"We can settle this war very simply! Choose a man and send him down here with me. If he kills me, Israel wins; if I kill him, the Philistines win! Very simple!"

A murmur broke out through the army of Israel. Who could ever kill this man?

"Israel! I challenge you! Send a man—if you have one!" Then Goliath went back up the hill to where the Philistine army stood. Saul and his army drew back further on their hill. They were terrified.

Every day after that, twice a day for forty days, Goliath approached and said the same thing.

The conversation in the army of Israel was always the same:

"Did you hear that?" they asked

each other. "Who'll take that challenge?"

"Easier to flatten this hill than kill that giant!"

Now David, whom Samuel had anointed and who played the harp for Saul, was there, listening to the soldiers.

"What reward," he said, "will there be for the man who kills this monster?"

"Surely the king will make that man rich," the soldiers answered, "and give him his own daughter to marry. But who can do it? Goliath would break the man like a twig!"

"So!" David continued. "Are you going to stand here and let that—that thing insult Israel? This is God's army! Why are we afraid?"

David's older brother, Eliab, was also in the army of Israel. When he heard David speaking he grew furious.

"What are you doing here, anyway? I wish you'd go back home and take care of father's sheep. I know you. You're stirring up trouble. All you want is to see a fight!"

"What did I do?" David answered. "Can't I even talk?" And David went on talking to the soldiers.

Word of what David was saying reached Saul, and he sent for David.

"What's all this I hear?" he asked.

"Put your worries away," David said. "I will go and fight Goliath."

"Don't be foolish!" Saul said. "You are just a boy. That giant has been a soldier for years. You're nothing but a dreamer if you think you can kill him."

"But," David insisted, "when I was caring for my father's sheep, bears and lions would try to attack them and I would save the sheep, and if the lions or bears attacked me I would kill them with my bare hands! I have killed lions and bears because God helped me. God will help me kill this giant, too!"

"Well—" Saul hesitated. "Well— maybe. I don't hear anyone else saying they want to fight. We don't have much choice.... All right! Go—and may God go with you!"

Then Saul grabbed David's arm.

"Here!" he said. "Take my armor. You deserve to wear the king's armor."

So David put on Saul's helmet and breastplate. But he felt as if he were in prison.

"I can't even walk in these things," he said. "I'm not used to wearing them." So he took the armor off. Then he bent down and picked up five

found a chance to talk with the king.

"Lord Saul," they said, "you should have a harpist to play for you when you are feeling bad."

"Yes. I think that might help. Do you know anyone who plays the harp?"

"There is a young man in Bethlehem who plays quite well. His name is David."

"Send for him!"

And so it was that David entered the palace of the king. Saul liked him. And David played the harp for Saul to soothe him when he felt bad.

Time would pass before David became king. But everything was now prepared: God had chosen David, Samuel had anointed him, and David was living in the palace.

David would be king. But much would happen before that.

David and Goliath

THE Philistines were one of the strongest enemies that Israel had. They had often fought with Israel and, more often than not, the Philistines had won.

Now the Philistines were preparing for war again. They brought their troops together at Shochoh. There they took possession of a hill. Saul, the king of Israel, also brought his army to that place and lined it up on a hill across from the Philistines. The two armies thus stood facing each other on the two hills with a small valley stretching between them.

One of the Philistine soldiers marched down the hill toward the army of Israel. The men of Israel shuddered when they saw him. He was over nine feet tall! His armor alone was heavier than any man in the army of Israel. On his head was a huge bronze helmet, and his shield was large enough to be a wagon wheel. His name was Goliath.

When he spoke it sounded like the roar of a lion, and the roar echoed back and forth across the valley.

"Israel! Why stand you there? I am a Philistine! You are slaves of Saul!"

It seemed as though the hills themselves shook with the sound of Goliath's voice.

"We can settle this war very simply! Choose a man and send him down here with me. If he kills me, Israel wins; if I kill him, the Philistines win! Very simple!"

A murmur broke out through the army of Israel. Who could ever kill this man?

"Israel! I challenge you! Send a man—if you have one!" Then Goliath went back up the hill to where the Philistine army stood. Saul and his army drew back further on their hill. They were terrified.

Every day after that, twice a day for forty days, Goliath approached and said the same thing.

The conversation in the army of Israel was always the same:

"Did you hear that?" they asked

God Prepares a New King

IN THE beginning Saul was a fine king. But little by little he began to change. As happens so often, power went to his head. He began to refuse to obey God, and because of this God turned against Saul.

The servants in the palace noticed a change in the king. He was moody all day and, worse yet, he was afraid of everything. Now, Saul was a giant of a man, head and shoulders taller than anyone in Israel. What a sad thing it was to see such a man afraid of his own shadow!

The servants talked among themselves:

"We must do something to soothe the king."

"Yes, he cannot go on this way."

"I have an idea. I know a young man who plays the harp very well. We should ask the king to bring him here."

"And the next time the king is in one of his bad moods, the young man can play the harp! That's a splendid idea! We'll ask the king the next chance we get."

About that same time, God was speaking to Samuel:

"I regret having made Saul king. He refuses to obey me. It is time to prepare for a new king."

"But, Lord," Samuel said, "if I do that, Saul will surely kill me."

"I will tell you what to do," God said. "Saul will not know. Take a calf and go to Bethlehem. There you will meet a man named Jesse. Tell him you have come to offer sacrifice. Then when you have offered the sacrifice, ask Jesse to bring his sons to you."

Samuel did as he was told. He sacrificed the calf in Bethlehem, and when he was finished he said to Jesse:

"Bring your sons to me."

Jesse brought Eliab first.

Eliab was a fine-looking man, and when Samuel saw him he thought, "This must be the one." But God said to Samuel:

"Do not pay any attention to what

81

the man looks like. I do not see as man sees. I look into the heart. This is not the one."

Samuel told Jesse that he wanted to see his other sons. Jesse brought nine more sons, but Samuel rejected them all one by one. Then he said, "Are these all of your sons?"

"There is one more," Jesse answered. "David. He is taking care of the sheep out on the hill. Probably playing his harp, too."

"Send for him," Samuel said.

When David came into sight, God said to Samuel:

"This is the one. Anoint him."

So, in front of the family, Samuel took oil and poured it on David's head. The spirit of God came upon David. But Samuel said no more.

In Saul's palace, the servants finally

smooth stones and put them in the little bag he had hanging from his belt. He drew out his slingshot and began to move toward the Philistine army. Goliath then stepped forward. He was almost twice David's size. He looked down at David.

"Ha! Ha! Ha!" Goliath's laughter roared through the valley. "What is this? Ha! Ha! Ha! I ask for a man and they send me a baby! I have no milk for you, little one. Go home! Ha! Ha! Ha! Ha! Ha!"

But David did not budge. "You come at me," he said, "with your enormous sword. But I come at you in the name of God, the God you have insulted. God will be my sword!"

"Come over here!" Goliath growled. "I'll feed you to the birds. Not much of a supper for them. Ha! But that seems to be all the great army of Israel has to offer!"

"I will kill you," David replied. "I'll feed *you* and all the Philistines to the birds. They'll have *plenty* to eat!"

"Oh, my! How the child can talk! All right, my tender little baby—come! Let's get this over with. I have no more time for talk!"

With that, David ran toward the giant. He drew a stone from his bag. He put it in his slingshot. He pulled his arm back. With all his strength, he flung the stone. The stone whistled through the air. It slammed into Goliath's forehead, and the thud resounded a thousand times throughout the valley.

"Agh!" Goliath screamed in pain, reaching for his head. Then he toppled like an enormous tree and crashed to the ground.

David ran to the fallen giant and, with Goliath's own sword, killed him.

A roar went up from the army of Israel. They dashed down the hill and up the other side after the Philistine army. They chased them for miles, killing many and wounding more.

All of Israel rejoiced that night. David, the shepherd boy, the harp player had, in the name of God, rescued Israel!

The Jealous King

AFTER David had killed Goliath he was the hero of Israel. Everywhere in the country people made up songs to sing about the great David. Even moody King Saul was happy. After all, David played the harp to soothe him whenever he was in one of his bad moods.

But then one day Saul heard some girls singing one of the songs about David:

"Saul killed thousands;
But David killed tens
of thousands."

And jealousy grew in Saul.

"What kind of a song is that to sing?" he thought. "They give tens of thousands to David but only thousands to me! Soon they'll want to make him king in my place!"

All that day Saul's mood grew blacker and blacker. The next day he was almost crazy with jealousy.

David was called to play the harp for Saul, to see if the music could break Saul's bad mood. But all the while David played, Saul fidgeted and kept toying with his spear. Suddenly, in a fit of rage, Saul jumped up and flung the spear at David. David jumped away just in time and escaped from the palace.

When Saul's bad mood finally did pass a few days later, Saul realized he had done wrong. The people of Israel loved David and David had only done good for the country. So Saul made David an officer in the army.

But David won battle after battle and Saul began to be jealous again. "These people!" he thought. "Will they never stop talking about David? What about me? What about King Saul? I know—I know. I will put a stop to this. I will send David to fight the Philistines and they will kill him!" He sent for David.

"I will give you my daughter, Merab, to marry," Saul said.

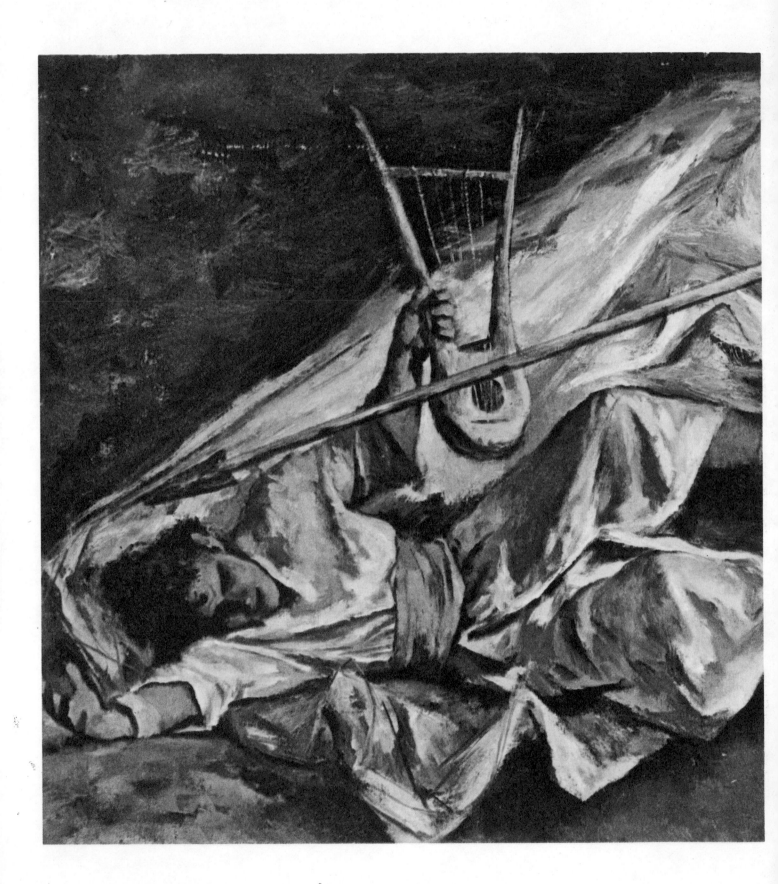

"But, my Lord King," David replied, "I am from a poor family. I am nothing. How could I hope to marry your daughter?"

"Don't worry about that. But—there is something you must do first."

"Yes, my lord?"

"You must lead the army against the Philistines and fight bravely. Then you can marry Merab."

David led the army in battle, but he was not killed, as Saul had wanted. Then Saul ignored the bargain he had made and let Merab marry another man.

Saul's other daughter, Michal, then came to him.

"David is sad because you forgot your promise, father. But he has no need to be. Merab never loved him. But I do! With all my heart! I want you to let me marry David."

"Fine!" Saul answered in a happy tone. (He was not really happy, but

he thought this was another chance to have David killed.) "I will arrange it!"

And Saul sent his servant to tell David that he could marry Michal.

"He must think me a fool," David said. "It will be the same as last time."

"No," the servant said. "Saul really loves you. He is serious about his promise."

"Anyway, I'm too poor to be the husband of a princess."

"That does not matter. Saul only wants you to kill a hundred Philistines."

"A hundred Philistines! Well—I do love Michal. Perhaps... Yes! It will be done!"

And that night David, went out with his men and killed two hundred Philistines. The whole country heard about it and so, this time, Saul was too embarrassed to go back on his promise. Michal became David's wife.

David's life was then happy for a time. Since David was his son-in-law, Saul forgot about trying to kill him. But David won more and more battles, and the people of Israel had David's name on their lips all day. The old jealousy began to rage in Saul again. When he could stand it no longer, he sent soldiers to David's house.

"Wait until the morning comes,"

he instructed them. "When David wakes up, kill him!"

But Michal heard about the plot and she warned David.

"You must escape tonight! They will try to kill you in the morning!"

So she helped David climb out the window, and he fled in the darkness.

Then Michal took a statue and put it in the bed. When the soldiers knocked on the door in the morning, she said, "David is in bed. He's ill."

The soldiers went back to Saul.

"What do I care if he's sick, you fools?" Saul shouted. "I want the man dead. Can't anyone do as King Saul says? Never mind! I'll kill him myself as he lies in bed!"

He ran to David's house and into the bedroom. "Now, my fine harpist," he raged, "you have played your last tune!" He whipped back the bed covers.

"Wha...? A statue! A statue! Will I never have peace?" He grabbed Michal and shook her. "How could you do this to me?" he roared. "My own daughter! You let my enemy escape!"

"But he told me he would kill me if I didn't let him go," Michal lied.

And so, David, the hero of Israel, had to leave Israel and hide from Saul. But, one day, he would return.

He would be king of Israel!

Two Friends

AFTER killing Goliath, David was popular with everyone in Israel. Everyone wants to be the friend of a hero. But from all of these people, David chose one very special friend. He was King Saul's son and his name was Jonathan. The two of them—David and Jonathan— became like blood brothers. Jonathan gave David his own cloak and sword. The two friends were seen together everywhere.

Then King Saul became jealous of David and wanted to have him killed. Jonathan always took David's part and tried to convince his father that he should not harm David. But King Saul was a moody man. One day he would agree with Jonathan, the next day he would order that David be killed. Finally it became too dangerous for David to stay in the palace and he had to go into hiding.

Jonathan went to David and tried to persuade him to return.

"My father's mood has changed," he said. "He will not kill you. Come back home."

"But tomorrow his mood will change again and he *will* kill me, Jonathan," David answered.

"No, David, it's different now. I know. Father always tells me everything."

"But, Jonathan, he knows we are friends. He won't tell you about this. He knows you would warn me."

"What can I do, then? You know that tomorrow is the day of the new moon. Father expects you to come back and take your place at the table with us."

David thought for a moment. "Tell him," he said, "that I went to Bethlehem to have a feast with my family. If he says 'fine,' then you know I am safe. But if he gets angry, then you'll know he still wants to kill me."

"All right, David. I promise. I'll find out what father is planning tomorrow and I'll let you know."

"But if he wants to kill me he'll be watching you. He won't let you warn me. How will you let me know?"

"That's a problem, isn't it?" Jonathan looked about for a moment, thinking. Suddenly he said, "Come, David, let's go over to that field there. I have an idea!"

The two of them ran to the field. Jonathan, out of breath, said:

"Here! This is a good spot. Tomorrow, at supper, I'll find out what father is going to do. Then the next morning I will come here."

"But your father's men will follow you!"

"No, David. I'll make it look like I'm coming here to practice shooting arrows. Do you see that pile of stones over there?"

"Yes."

"You hide behind those stones, and I'll pretend that I'm trying to hit them. I'll send my servant after the arrows. If I tell him the arrows are off to the side, then you'll know everything is safe and you can come home. But if I say the arrow is in front of him, then you'll know you must escape."

"To the side—come home," David repeated. "To the front—escape."

"Right!"

The two shook hands and

Jonathan went back to the palace.

The next evening the king's family was seated at the table. David's place was empty.

"Where's David?" King Saul asked. "He was supposed to come."

"Oh," Jonathan answered, "he had to go to Bethlehem. His family is having a feast. He asked to be excused."

"You miserable wretch!" Saul raged. "Don't you think I know you're hand in glove with that son of Jesse? You think I'm blind? Wake up, you fool! As long as David lives you can never be sure of becoming king! The people will want to make David king! Now go and get him! I condemn him to death!"

"But why?" Jonathan asked. "Why should David die? What has he done?"

Saul picked up his spear and threatened Jonathan with it.

"What's this? You want to kill me, too?" Jonathan got up and stormed out of the room.

The next morning Jonathan went out to the field with his servant. He shot an arrow into the air.

"Go fetch it," he shouted to his servant. The servant ran after the arrow.

"No! Not there! It's up in front of you! Up in front!"

From behind the rocks David

heard Jonathan's shouts and he knew that he must escape. But Jonathan gave the servant the bow and the rest of the arrows and told him to return home. When the servant was out of sight, Jonathan went closer to the rocks.

"Careful!" David whispered from behind the rocks.

"I don't care," Jonathan answered. "We cannot be separated without even saying good-by. We may never see each other again. I don't care who sees."

David came from behind the rocks and they gave each other a manly embrace.

"Good-by, good friend," Jonathan said. "May God go with you. God knows that our friendship will never die." Then Jonathan turned and went home.

The two great friends met only once again—in a town called Ziph— and that was only for a very short time. A little while after that Jonathan was killed in a battle against the Philistines.

But the story of their friendship still lives.

The Massacre

AVID went from one hiding place to another. King Saul's men were always after him. The king had sent them to kill David and they were determined to carry out the order! Of course, being on the run all the time, David had a difficult time getting food. One day, when he was especially hungry, he went to the town of Nob and cautiously entered the house of the priest, Ahimelech.

When Ahimelech saw David, he said, "David, what are you doing here? Why are you alone? Where are your soldiers?" Ahimelech did not know that Saul wanted to have David killed. He thought David was still an officer in the army.

David answered, "I'm on a secret mission for the king. I will meet my men later in another town. But right now I need something to eat. Do you have any bread?"

"Well—I have the five loaves of bread we offer to God every day. I suppose you can have them."

"They will be fine." David took the loaves and began to leave. Then he turned back to Ahimelech. "Oh—one other thing. I had to run out so fast that I didn't have time to take my sword. Do you have a sword or a spear I could use?"

"Why—yes. I have a sword that you know very well, David. It is Goliath's sword. We have kept it here ever since you killed that giant! Here!" Ahimelech took the enormous sword and gave it to David. "No man deserves to carry this sword more than you," he said.

"That will be perfect. Thank you."

David turned to leave. As he was walking out, he thought he heard someone move in the next room. He stopped. No sound. He shrugged. "I must be hearing things," he thought, and left Ahimelech's house.

A short time later, in the king's palace, Saul was again in a rage.

"You are all against me!" he shouted at his men. "What is it that David gives you that makes you help

him? No one can find him. No one knows where he is! What is he—a ghost?"

One of Saul's servants, a man named Doeg, spoke up.

"I saw David just a few days ago."

"Where?" Saul demanded.

"In Nob," Doeg said. "He went to Ahimelech's house. I know. I was in the other room when he got there. And Ahimelech gave him food and Goliath's sword."

"See! Even the priests are against me! We'll see about that! Bring me that priest and his family!"

And Ahimelech and his whole family, including relatives, were summoned into Saul's presence. When Saul saw them, he shouted:

"Ahimelech! Why are you against me?"

"But..." Ahimelech shuddered. "What does the king mean?"

"You helped David! That's what I mean!"

"But—but David is your greatest warrior. No one serves you better than David. Of course I helped David. How could I refuse?"

"David is my enemy!"

"Your enemy? Your enemy? But how—"

"You will die, Ahimelech! And your whole family!" Saul turned to his guards. "Put this priest and his whole family to death!"

But the guards hesitated. They did not want to kill a priest.

"Will no one obey me? Doeg—you do it!"

And Doeg obeyed Saul. The only one who escaped the massacre was a son, named Ahitub. He ran from the palace and all the way to where David was hiding. He told David what had happened.

"What misery!" David exclaimed. "I thought there was someone in the other room the day I visited your father. All this because of me! When will Saul stop? Ahitub, you stay with me. I will keep you safe. I swear to it. They will have to kill me before they kill you!"

And so Ahitub joined up with David. Later, others joined him, until David had a group of about three hundred.

Now, if Saul came, they would be ready!

David Spares Saul's Life

DAVID and his men are camped in Engedi!'' a servant told King Saul. "Good! This time we will get him! Get three thousand men ready. We will march after David! We will finally rid Israel of that harp player!"

So a small army, headed by Saul, set out after David. They searched the region of Engedi but could not find a trace of David. Then, one hot day, Saul went into a cave to cool himself off. He did not know that David and his men were hidden in that very same cave!

David's men said to him, "This is your chance, David. God has put Saul into your hands! He is alone. Kill him!"

David took his sword and crept through the black cave like a cat. Without a sound he reached Saul. He was so close that he could reach out and touch him. He held up his sword. But instead of killing Saul, he bent over and cut a piece of white cloth from the bottom of the king's robe. Saul never heard a sound! Then David returned to his men.

"Did you do it?" they whispered.

"I cut a piece from his robe," David answered.

"Cut a piece from his robe! Why didn't you kill him? He would have killed you!"

"But he is the king of Israel," David explained. "Anointed by God to be king! I could never kill the man God has chosen!"

"But why the piece of his robe?"

"You will see."

Just then they heard Saul moving out of the cave. David hurried after him. When Saul had gone a little way out, David came out after him.

"My Lord King!" David shouted across the rocks to Saul. "Why do you listen to those who say I want to harm you? Look at this!" And David held up the piece of white cloth. Saul looked down and saw that it had been cut from his own robe!

"Do you see?" David continued. "I

could have killed you just now—but I did not! I have never harmed you— nor will I! Why do you hunt me like an animal?"

"Is that really you, David?" Saul asked.

"Yes, my lord!"

"You are a better man than I, David. And you have proved it today. God put me in your power and you did not kill me! I will hunt you no longer! You are free!"

And Saul called his men and returned home. But David stayed in hiding. He knew that Saul was a moody man and often forgot his promises. And David was right! Several times Saul did send men after David again to kill him. But no one could capture David.

So it happened that David had to continue living in hiding. But God had not forgotten David. Long before, He had chosen David to be the new king of Israel. Saul had offended God too deeply.

One day, in a battle with the Philistines, Saul was wounded and about to be captured. He drew his own sword and fell on it, killing himself. It was the same battle in which Jonathan, Saul's son and David's friend, died.

And so the reign of Saul ended. He who had sought David with the sword for so many years, now himself died by the same sword.

At last, David was free. And more than free—he was now the king of Israel!

Solomon and Adonijah

DAVID was the finest king that Israel ever had. He was not perfect—only God is perfect. But, in general, Israel was a happy country while David was king. But when David became very old people began to worry. Who would be the new king?

Two of David's sons wanted to be king, Adonijah and Solomon. David had decided on Solomon and, of course, Adonijah was not happy about his father's decision.

"My father is an old, old man," he told some friends. "I don't think he knows what is happening any more. I have a plan."

"What is it?" the friends asked.

"My father has not told the people yet who his choice for king is..I will make the choice for him."

"But what about Solomon?"

"Only a few of us know that my father has chosen Solomon. The people don't know. Now—I will make myself king! Father is too old to know what is happening. The people will believe I am king. Then we can get rid of Solomon. We'll tell the people Solomon was planning treason against me. What do you think?"

"But...but..."

"Come on now! Let's have no doubts. You'll all be rich men in a short time! Let's get busy. I'll need a fine chariot and a troop of men to run in front of the chariot. Then we'll have a great feast and a sacrifice."

All these things were done and, just as Adonijah had said, the people believed he must surely be king. They were not happy, because they liked Solomon better. But they accepted Adonijah.

When Bathsheba, Solomon's mother, heard what was happening, she went to David.

"David, my lord," she said, "you promised that Solomon would be king. But Adonijah is riding all over in his chariot telling everyone *he* is king! And the people believe him! And—and you don't know anything about it!"

106

"Make him ride to Gehon. There the priests must anoint him. Then bring Solomon back to the palace. Have him sit on my throne. Then have the servants play the trumpets and shout: 'Long live King Solomon.' The people will then know that it is my decision: Solomon will be king!"

All this was done, and the people believed. "Long live King Solomon!" they shouted. And they were so happy that Solomon was king and not Adonijah that they celebrated all over the country. In the king's city there was singing and shouting and dancing.

Adonijah was eating supper with his friends when he heard the shouting outside.

"What's all that noise?" he asked.

At that moment a man came in the door.

"Solomon is king!" he shouted.

"What do you mean—*Solomon* is king? *I* am king!"

"No. Your father had Solomon ride the king's mule and be anointed, and now he is sitting on the king's throne. Solomon is king!"

Adonijah looked around at his friends, very worried. "The worst has happened," he said. "I—I didn't think my father could do it." One look at Adonijah's face told his friends that it was all over for them. They fled out of the house. Adonijah ran, too—from the house straight to the Temple. He

"Ah," David muttered, "must I have such pain in my last days?"

"Adonijah thinks you can't do anything any more! He thinks you are too old even to think!"

"Adonijah is wrong!" David said. "I am old, but I have not lost my mind. We must do something to show the people that Adonijah is not king. Here, listen! This is what you must do. Take my mule—the king's mule— make Solomon ride it."

107

was afraid that Solomon would have him killed. But he was safe in the Temple. No one—not even the king—could kill a man in the Temple. It was against the law.

But Solomon made his first wise decision as king. He sent word to Adonijah that he would not be killed. Adonijah was to go home and not cause any more trouble.

When David felt he was about to die, he called Solomon to him.

"Be a man," he instructed Solomon. "Rule the people well. Keep God's laws. Never forget God and you will be successful in whatever you do."

A short time later, David died. Israel mourned its greatest king. The shepherd boy, the harp player who killed the mighty giant Goliath, the great soldier, the kind king, had died. He had gone to God.

Now Solomon must follow in his father's footsteps.

Solomon's Wisdom

WHEN Solomon was a young king, God appeared to him in a dream.

"Solomon," God said, "what would you like Me to give you?"

Solomon thought for a moment, then said:

"My Lord God, you always showed great kindness to my father and he was able to rule Israel well. But I'm so young—and here I am, king of all these people. Sometimes I don't know which way to turn. I think the most important thing I need is wisdom. I need an understanding mind, so I can tell right from wrong."

"I am very happy with your answer," God said. "You did not ask for riches or honor, but only for wisdom. Well, I will give you wisdom, and riches and honor besides."

Then Solomon woke up.

A short time later two women came to Solomon. They wanted him to settle a fight they were having.

"Lord King," one woman said, "this woman and I live in the same house. Not long ago I had a baby."

"And three days later," the second woman said, "I had a baby, too."

"Now," the first woman continued, "there was no one else in the house—just the two of us. And one night while we were sleeping, she rolled over in her bed and killed her child."

"Not so!" the other women cried.

"Yes, it is! And then you got up and put your dead baby in my bed and took my baby. And when I woke up, Lord King, to give my baby some milk—he was dead! But in the morning I looked at the baby more closely and I saw what she had done. It was her baby that was dead!"

"That's not true, King Solomon! My baby is alive and hers is dead!"

"Bah! That's a lie! The live baby

is mine!"

"That's what you say!"

And the two women went on squabbling until the palace rocked with their shouting. Solomon just sat there, his chin in his hand, listening to them—and thinking. Finally he called to his servant:

"Bring me a sword."

The servant ran out and brought a large, sharp sword.

"Now," Solomon said, "cut the baby in two. That's the only way we can settle this! Each woman can have half!"

One women was horrified! "Oh, no, King Solomon!" she cried. "Give her the child. It is mine—but let her have it! Dear God, don't kill the child."

But the other woman shouted, "No! Neither of us will have the child! Go ahead! Do it! Cut him up!"

Solomon held up his hand. "No," he said quietly. "Do not touch the child. Give him to this woman who did not want him killed. She is certainly his mother!"

And news of Solomon's decision went throughout all of Israel. And everyone agreed: there was no man alive who was wiser than King Solomon!

The Prophet Elijah

APROPHET is a man of God—a messenger God sends to tell people how He feels about the way the world is going. There are many prophets mentioned in the Bible. One of the greatest was Elijah.

Elijah lived in a time when Ahab was king of Israel. It was a time when many people had forgotten God and begun to worship false gods. One false god they especially worshiped was called Baal.

Naturally, God was displeased with the people. He sent a drought on Israel, so that the country had no rain. In the morning there was not even any dew on the ground. Elijah had warned King Ahab that this would happen, but Ahab paid no attention.

But God protected Elijah.

"Go to a brook called Cherith, which is near the river Jordan," God said to Elijah. "You can drink water from the brook, and I will send ravens to you with food."

Elijah did as he was told, and it was as God had said. In the morning ravens brought Elijah bread, and in the evening they brought him meat. And, in the beginning, Elijah had plenty of water to drink in the brook. But after a while the brook dried up. The whole countryside became as hard as an old crust of bread.

"Go to Zarephath now," God said to Elijah. "A widow there will give you food to eat."

So Elijah set out again. When he reached the entrance to the city of Zarephath, he saw a woman picking up sticks.

"Could you please bring me a cup of water?" Elijah said to the woman.

"Just a minute," she said and walked off to get the water.

Elijah called after her, "And could I have a crust of bread, too?"

The woman turned and said, "Honestly, sir, I don't have any bread. Do you know what I was

just doing? I have only a little handful of flour left in a jar and a few drops of cooking oil in a jug. I was just picking up sticks to make a fire. I am going to make a little cake for my son and myself. I have no husband. He is dead. My son and I will eat the cake, and that will be the end of the food. Then—then we will die, too."

"Don't worry, my good woman," Elijah said. "I am a man of God, and God has promised that your jar will never be empty of flour nor your jug empty of oil until the rains return to Israel."

"But—how is that possible?"

"Nothing is impossible for God. Now go. First make a cake for me. Then you will see that you have plenty flour and oil to make cakes for yourself and your son."

"My!" The woman was still doubtful but she went to make the cakes and, sure enough, there was plenty left for her and her son. In fact, no matter how much she cooked, she never got to the bottom of the jar or the jug!

But a short time later the woman's son became sick and each day he grew worse until, one day, the woman saw that he was no longer breathing.

"Oh!" she cried to Elijah with her dead son in her lap. "Man of God, what wrong did I ever do to you? Did you come here to pay me for my old sins? Did you come to kill my son?"

And the woman wrung her hands and cried and carried on as if she were going out of her mind.

Elijah said quietly, "Give me your son." And he took her son from her lap and brought him upstairs to where Elijah had his own bed. He put the boy down on the bed and then called to God:

"Dear God, this woman has looked after me all this time. Will you now send her this sorrow as payment?"

Then he stretched himself three times over the body of the boy and called out again:

"Dear God, bring life back to this child! I beg you!"

And God heard Elijah. Slowly the color came back into the boy's cheeks and his eyes blinked open.

"What happened?" the boy said.

"Never mind," Elijah answered. "Come!"

And he brought the boy down the stairs.

"Look!" he said to the woman, "your son is alive and well!"

The woman let out a shriek of surprise and joy. "Oh, Elijah! Now I know you are a man of God. Now I know you are truly a prophet!"

Elijah
and the Priests of Baal

IT DID not rain in Israel for more than three years. The ground was like stone and the grass as yellow as straw. King Ahab was worried about his animals. He called his servant, Obadiah.

"Obadiah, you must look for water all over the country. Because of that prophet, Elijah, everything is dried up around here. It was he who brought this curse on Israel. See if you can't find a brook or a stream that hasn't dried up yet. There must be grass somewhere for the cattle to eat and water to drink. You go one way and I'll go the other. We must find water!"

And so they set out, King Ahab in one direction and Obadiah in the other. In a short time whom should Obadiah meet but Elijah!

"Elijah!" Obadiah exclaimed.

"Yes, it is I," Elijah said. "I want you to go to Ahab and tell him I am here. God has told me He will bring rain to Israel again."

"Tell Ahab?" Obadiah said. "But you must be joking! Ahab would kill

me. He thinks you are the cause of the drought. He's been looking for you everywhere, but no one can ever find you. God always whisks you off to some hiding place. I can just see it now. I go and tell Ahab you are here, and when he comes you have disappeared into thin air again—like you always do! He'll kill me, I tell you!"

"Go and tell him," Elijah insisted.

"But, Elijah, you know I am a good man. I've always been good to the prophets. Remember how I hid fifty of them from Ahab in a cave and fed them at the risk of my own neck? Now you want me to be killed?"

"No—you have my promise. I will stay here. I will not disappear."

"All right. But remember—you promised!"

And Obadiah went in search of King Ahab, looking back over his shoulder now and then to see if Elijah was still standing there.

And Ahab came to see Elijah.

"So there you are, you miserable

115

wretch!" Ahab shouted when he saw Elijah. "The wretch who brought all this misery to Israel!"

"Not I, Ahab," Elijah replied. "I did not bring this misery on Israel. You did! You have forgotten God and gone off to worship that ugly idol, Baal. It is your fault that God has stopped the rains in Israel. But God will have an end to all this! Tell the people of Israel to gather at Mount Carmel. And send for four hundred priests of Baal. We shall see who the true God of Israel is!"

Ahab obeyed Elijah because he feared him. The people gathered at Mount Carmel, and four hundred priests of Baal also. Elijah walked up in front of the people.

"How long," he said, "are you people going to continue jumping from one foot to the other? First, you choose God and then Baal and then God and then Baal. Listen! If the God of Israel is truly God—follow Him! If Baal is god—follow *him*! Which one is it to be?"

But the people were silent. The only sound was the echo of Elijah's voice on the mountain.

"Don't you have any tongues?" Elijah continued. "All right—listen, then, and watch! I can see you have ears and eyes! I am the only prophet of God here. Look over there! You can see at least four hundred priests of Baal, shuffling their feet over there!"

The people were still silent.

"Now! Bring me two bulls. Kill them and prepare them for sacrifice. Give one to the priests of Baal. Now—

you priests of Baal! Take the bull and put it on your altar and put wood under it. But don't set the wood on fire! The true God will provide the fire."

The people finally broke their silence. "Agreed!" they shouted.

And the priests of Baal prepared the altar. Then from morning to noon they called to their god with their arms outstretched. "Oh, Baal—send fire! Answer us!" When there was no answer they began a dance around the altar, hopping from one foot to the other.

At noon Elijah called to them:

"Shout a little louder! After all, Baal is a god. He may be busy! Or maybe he went on a trip. Who knows—maybe he's asleep!"

And the priests shouted louder and louder. But still there was no answer. Not the slightest wisp of smoke came from their altar.

When the sun started going down, Elijah finally said:

"Enough of this foolishness! Come! We will build an altar to the God of Israel. Bring me twelve stones. Israel has twelve tribes, so we will have a stone for each tribe....Fine! Now—build the altar!...Good, good! That will do. Now, dig a trench around the altar."

The people dug a large trench around the altar. Then they put wood under the altar and the bull on top of it.

"Bring me water," Elijah commanded, "lots of it.... There, now drench the altar and the wood with the water!"

The water splashed over the altar and ran down into the trench. The wood was soaked.

"Do it again!" Elijah said.

This time the trench almost overflowed with water.

"Again!"

Elijah now came closer and saw that everything was thoroughly drenched. Then he looked up to heaven and said:

"God of Abraham and Isaac and Israel—let these people know today

that You are their God. Send your fire!"

And immediately, with a thunderous blast, fire hit the altar. The bull was burnt to a crisp in a second and the wood turned to ashes. Even the water rose as steam into the air!

When the people saw this, they fell on the ground and began screaming:

"The God of Israel is the true God! The God of Israel is the true God!"

And Elijah shouted over the din:

"Go home and eat! I hear rain coming in the distance! And never— NEVER!—never forget God again!"

Elisha

ELISHA was an assistant to Elijah. When Elijah was old he was taken up into heaven in a fiery chariot, and as he went his cloak fell to the ground. Elisha picked up the cloak. This was a sign from God that Elisha would now be the prophet of Israel.

One day, when Elisha was on a journey, a woman in the town of Shunem invited him to stay in her house and eat. And, after that, whenever Elisha passed by that way he would stop at the woman's house. One day the woman said to her husband:

"Dear, I am sure that Elisha is a man of God—a prophet. Why don't we build a room for him on the roof and put a bed in it and a table and a chair and a lamp. That way, whenever he stops here he'll have his own room."

Her husband had the room built and the furniture moved in. When Elisha came he was very pleased with their kindness, and he always used the room when he was in that part of the country. One day, after he had rested in the room, he said to his servant, Gehazi:

"Gehazi, go down to the woman of the house and ask her if there is anything I can do for her. Can I ask a favor for her from the king or from some general?"

Gehazi went down and asked the woman, but she said, "No, thank you. I am quite content."

Gehazi gave Elisha the answer.

"But," Elisha said, "there must be something we can do for her. She has been very kind."

"I have a suggestion," Gehazi said to Elisha.

"What is that!"

"Well, I've noticed that her husband is old and that they don't have any children."

"Good, Gehazi! Call the woman!"

The woman came up to the room and stood at the door. Elisha said, "Next year at this time you will have your own child in your arms."

"Oh, Elisha! Don't tell me stories

like that. You know we can't have any children."

"You will see," Elisha smiled.

And the next year, just as Elisha had said, the woman gave birth to a son.

When the child grew a little older, he used to work on the farm with his father. One day, out in the field, he turned to his father and said:

"My head hurts." Then he clenched his head in his hands. "Ow! My head."

His father did not think it was very serious, but he told one of the farmhands to carry the boy to his mother. The farmhand did so and laid the boy in his mother's arms. But he grew worse and at noon he died. She took the body upstairs and put it in Elisha's bed. She did not tell her husband what had happened but only sent word to him that she was going to see Elisha.

Elisha was at Mount Carmel at the time, and when he saw the woman coming toward him, he said to Gehazi:

"Here comes the woman from Shunem. Run and ask her if everything is all right."

But the woman would not anwer Gehazi. She went straight to Elisha and told him her son was dead.

"Here!" Elisha said to Gehazi. "Quickly now! No talking to anyone on the way. Take my cane and run to the child and stretch the cane over him."

Gehazi ran off.

"You may go," Elisha said to the woman. "Everything will be all right."

"No," the woman said, "I will not go, Elisha, unless you go, too!"

"All right," Elisha answered. "We will go together."

While they were on their way, Gehazi came running back toward them.

"I stretched the cane over the boy," he said, out of breath. "Just as you said! But nothing happened!"

Elisha then went into the house. He went into his room, shut the door, and prayed to God. Then he stretched himself on top of the child. The boy's body grew warm.

After this Elisha came down from his room and walked around inside the house. He did this seven times. After the seventh time, the boy sneezed and opened his eyes.

Elisha called the woman, "Here is your son! Come, and take him!"

The mother thanked the man of God and folded the child in her arms.

Elisha Cures Naaman

THE chief of the Syrian army at that time was a man called Naaman. He was a fine general, and the king of Syria treated him with respect. Naaman therefore had fame and riches—but he had a problem that ruined his happiness. He had a disease called leprosy.

Naaman's wife had as a servant a little girl from Israel. One day she said to her mistress:

"I wish Naaman would go and visit Elisha, the prophet. I am sure Elisha would cure his leprosy."

Naaman's wife told him this, and Naaman mentioned it to the king.

"Well, go to Israel," the king said. "I'll write a letter of introduction to the Israeli king for you."

So Naaman packed up for the trip. He took $20,000 in silver and $60,000 in gold and ten rich robes. He would give these as gifts to the prophet if he were cured.

Naaman and his men went directly to the king of Israel and gave him the letter of introduction. The king opened it and read:

WITH THIS LETTER I AM
SENDING YOU MY ARMY CHIEF,
NAAMAN, SO THAT YOU MAY
CURE HIM OF HIS LEPROSY.
KING OF SYRIA

The king of Israel was enraged when he read these words.

"What's this?" he exclaimed. "Do you think I am God? That I can give life and take it away? What a terrible thing! I know what your king is trying to do. He's trying to stir up trouble so he can start a war with us!"

But Elisha heard people talking about what had happened in the palace. He sent word to the king:

"Don't be upset. Send Naaman to me. He will see that I am a true prophet!"

So Naaman and his men came to Elisha's house. When he saw Naaman outside the door, Elisha said to Gehazi:

"Go out and tell Naaman to

bathe in the Jordan River seven times."

Gehazi brought the message.

"What do you mean?" Naaman exploded in anger. "I came all this way and he won't even come out to see me! What is this? Bathe in the Jordan! We have perfectly good rivers in Syria—better than your muddy old Jordan! If I can be cured by bathing in a river, I can do that very well at home, thank you! Good-by!"

Naaman stomped off in a huff. But his men tried to reason with him.

"Naaman..."

"Don't talk to me! I've never been so insulted in my life!"

"But, listen. Just one moment!

124

What if Elisha asked you to do
something really hard—would you
have done it?"

"Of course I would. But he…"

"Then, why won't you bathe in
the Jordan? What harm will it do
you?"

"I…I…"

"Come on! It'll only take a
minute!"

"Well—all right."

So they went to the Jordan and
Naaman plunged into the water
seven times. And when he came out
the seventh time his skin was as
clean and as fresh as the skin of a
child!

They all returned to Elisha's
house. This time Elisha let Naaman
come into the house.

125

"Now I know," Naaman said to Elisha, "that there is no other real God except the God of Israel. Please—take the gifts I have brought you."

"No," Elisha said, "I serve God. I cannot accept your gifts."

"But I have silver and gold, and..."

"No."

"Well...if you insist. But I promise I will worship no other God than the God of Israel."

"You will do well," Elisha replied. "Now go in peace."

When Naaman had been gone only a few minutes, Elisha's servant thought to himself:

"Why should Elisha let Naaman go off with all those gifts? I'm going to get some of those things for myself."

And Gehazi ran after Naaman. When the army chief saw him coming, he stopped and called, "Is everything all right?"

"Yes," Gehazi answered. "But Elisha sent me to tell you that two students just arrived at the house. He'd like you to leave $2,000 and some robes for them."

"Why, certainly! Anything! Here—take $4,000 and these robes....You two men, there! Help Gehazi carry these things."

Gehazi started back to Elisha's house with the men. But before he reached it, he sent the two men back to Naaman and then hid the gifts in his own house. Later, he returned to Elisha.

"Gehazi," Elisha, "where have you been?"

"Nowhere," Gehazi lied.

"Gehazi, don't you know I could see you in my mind when you were talking to Naaman? Well, now you are rich. You can buy anything you want."

"Yes, Elisha!"

"But!"

"Yes?"

"Naaman's leprosy will now be yours!"

And Gehazi left the house—a leper!

A Prophet Without Mercy

"JONAH," God said, "go to the great city of Nineveh. I want you to tell the people there that I see the evil they are doing. Tell them that I will punish them."

Jonah did not answer. He knew that he was a prophet and that it was his duty to carry God's message wherever God wanted him to. "But," he thought to himself, "the people in Nineveh are not Hebrews. They are foreigners. And I know God. He's too good. He'll find some way to forgive those foreigners. I don't see why God should help them. Aren't the Hebrews enough for Him?"

So Jonah decided to run away from God. Instead of going to Nineveh, he would go to the most distant city he could think of. He would go to Tarshish. God wouldn't find him there. So Jonah went to Joppa, and there he found a ship going to Tarshish. He paid his fare and got on the ship.

Of course, it was foolish of Jonah to think that he could run away from God. No sooner was the ship out of sight of the shore than God sent a roaring, violent storm on the sea. The waves tossed the ship about like a piece of paper—up, down, around and around.

The sailors on the ship were frightened. They had never seen a storm like this one. They began to pray for help to their own gods. But the storm continued. Then they began throwing crates of goods overboard to lighten the ship.

When they went down in the ship to get the heavier crates, they found Jonah there—sleeping peacefully!

"What's this?" they yelled at Jonah.

"Eh?" Jonah began to open his eyes.

"Who can sleep in a storm like this? Get up! You'd better pray to your God, if you have one. We need all the help we can get!"

And still the storm raged. Great waves burst over the bow and foam

sizzled across the deck.

Then the sailors decided to cast lots to see who was the cause of the storm. Of course, the lot fell to Jonah.

"Who are you?" the sailors asked him. "Where are you from?"

"I am Jonah. I come from Israel."

" And what have you done to bring this storm on us?"

"I...I..."

"Well—say it! What have you done?"

"I'm running away from God. I'm a prophet, you see, and I should be doing God's work. But I don't want to."

The sailors looked at each other in terror. "We're lost, for sure!" they said.

"God is sending this storm," Jonah said. "It is my fault."

"What can we do to please your God?" the sailors asked. "What'll make Him stop the storm?"

Jonah hesitated a moment, then said slowly, "Throw me overboard."

"What! We're good sailors. We take care of our passengers."

"Yes," others said. "We don't throw them into the sea! Besides, you say you are a prophet. If we kill you, we'll be in a worse stew with your God! No, thanks! One storm is enough!"

"Throw me into the sea," Jonah repeated quietly.

"No," they answered. "We'll try to head the ship back to shore."

And the sailors set to work. With all their strength they tried to turn the ship, but the wind blew harder and the ship shook as if it were going to split into pieces. Finally, the sailors saw it was useless. Only one thing could be done. They spoke to God:

"God of the Hebrews, don't hold this against us. We don't want to kill Jonah. But we have no other choice!"

And they took Jonah and threw him into the sea. Immediately, the sea grew as calm as a lake on a bright summer's day. The sailors were astounded. They looked into the water—but Jonah was nowhere in sight! But they did notice a huge fish moving away from the ship. They sighed in relief and made a sacrifice of thanks to the God of Israel.

What they did not know was that God had sent the huge fish and it had swallowed Jonah alive! And Jonah lived three days and three nights in the belly of the fish!

Then Jonah prayed to God:

"My God, help me. I was wrong! I should not have run away from You. I am sorry. But You have saved me from the storm. Now help me again— and I will do what You want."

God heard Jonah's prayer and spoke to the fish. The fish went towards land, and there Jonah came tumbling out on the beach!

"Now get up!" God commanded Jonah. "Go to Nineveh and tell the people My message."

This time Jonah obeyed. Nineveh was an enormous city. It took three days to walk from one end of it to the other. Jonah walked through the city for one day and then began to preach.

"Only forty days left! Only forty days left! Nineveh will be destroyed in forty days!"

"What is this you are saying?" the people asked.

"ONLY FORTY DAYS LEFT!" And then Jonah explained what God had told him. To Jonah's surprise, the people began to change their lives. Even the king, when he heard what Jonah had said, made a law that all the people should do penance for their sins. And all of the city stopped doing evil.

God saw this change and forgave the people of Nineveh. He did not destroy the city.

Jonah was furious. "I knew it!" he said to God. "I *knew* it! It's just like I thought when You first told me to come here. That's why I tried to escape to Tarshish. I know You! You're too kind! You're too good! I knew You would forgive these people. They were evil—You should destroy them! But oh, no—You have to be kind! Agh! I'd rather be dead!"

"Jonah," God said, "do you think it's right to be angry about what I've done?"

"Yes, I do!" Jonah pouted. And he stomped to the outskirts of the city and sat down in a little hut to watch what would happen to the city. He was hoping God would change His mind. He grumbled to himself all day.

The hut was very rickety and the hot sun beamed in through it onto the top of Jonah's head. Of course, this made Jonah even grumpier. But God had a plant grow very fast and cover the hut with large leaves. The plant made Jonah feel much more comfortable and he grew very fond of it.

But the next day God sent a worm that ate into the plant and killed it. The leaves dried up and the sun came pouring through again. Jonah's face was soon covered with sweat. Jonah was furious again.

"I might as well be dead!" he complained to God.

"Are you angry, Jonah?" God asked.

"Yes!"

"About a plant?"

"Yes!"

"Do you think that is right?"

"Yes! Yes! Yes! I have every right to be angry!"

"You're very angry about a plant, Jonah. You feel sorry for a plant."

"I've got a right to feel sorry about my plant. It shaded me from the sun."

"But you did nothing to make the plant grow, Jonah."

"Agh!"

"Jonah, if you feel sorry about a plant, why can't I feel sorry for a city where thousands of people live?"

Jonah could not answer. God was right.

The Fiery Furnace

NEBUCHADNEZZAR, the king of Babylon, was very powerful. He was so powerful, in fact, that he thought he could make his own god. He had a golden statue made that was ninety feet high and nine feet wide. Then he told the people:

"I will have some musicians play some music. Every time they play, you must fall down flat on the ground and worship the golden statue I have made. Anyone who disobeys will be thrown immediately into a fiery furnace."

Naturally, no one wanted to die in the fiery furnace, so when the music started everyone fell down and worshiped the statue.

Everyone except the Jews!

Years before, Nebuchadnezzar had fought a war in Israel and brought many Jews back to Babylon as captives. Three of these Jews—Shadrach, Meshach, and Abednego—were very intelligent and became powerful in the government of Babylon. But Shadrach, Meshach, and Abednego never forgot that they were Jews and that there was only one true God. So they refused to fall down and worship the golden statue.

Some people went to the king and said, "O great king, you made a law that when the music starts everyone must fall down and worship the golden statue."

"Yes, I did."

"Everyone?"

"Everyone!"

"And if anyone disobeys they will be thrown into the fiery furnace. Is that right?"

"Yes, it is."

"Anyone?"

"What are these questions? Yes, anyone!"

"Well—there are three Jews in your very own government who refuse to worship."

Nebuchadnezzar's face grew bright red. "What! Who are they?"

"Shadrach, Meshach, and Abednego!"

"How dare they disobey my law!"

"They say there is only one God—so they can't worship your god."

"Send them to me at once! We'll see about their God!"

So Shadrach, Meshach, and Abednego were brought to the king.

''What is this I hear?'' Nebuchadnezzar asked in a rage. "Will you worship the statue or not?"

''No, we will not,'' Shadrach, Meshach, and Abednego answered. "We have the one true God."

Nebuchadnezzar jumped to his feet. "You will be thrown into the fiery furnace! What will your God do for you then?"

"Our God has the power to save us. But even if He does not save us, we will not disobey Him. We will not worship other gods."

"Fools!" Nebuchadnezzar shouted. "Guards! Guards! Get the furnace ready! I want it seven times hotter than usual! Seven times!"

The huge furnace was heated, and Shadrach, Meshach, and Abednego were bound with ropes.

"Now—into the furnace!" Nebuchadnezzar screamed.

The furnace was so hot that the flames leapt out when the door was opened and burned to death the guards who were holding Shadrach, Meshach, and Abednego. But finally the three Jewish men were pushed into the furnace and the door slammed behind them. Nebuchadnezzar could look through a window into the furnace and see the flames flaring around the three Jewish men. Suddenly, he jumped to his feet.

"Didn't we throw *three* men into the furnace?" he asked his attendants.

"Yes, we did."

"Well—look! I see *four*! Look at them! They're skipping around in there as if they were having a dance!"

Nebuchadnezzar moved as close to the furnace as he could and shouted:

"Shadrach, Meshach, and Abednego, come out!"

So the three men walked out of the fire. Not a hair on their heads was burned! Even their clothes were as perfect as when they were thrown into the furnace!

"God sent His angel to save us," they said.

Nebuchadnezzar was astounded. "I now make a new law!" he said. "Anyone whoever talks against the God of Shadrach, Meshach, and Abednego will be killed and his house will be torn down! Blessed be the God of Shadrach, Meshach, and Abednego!"

And Shadrach, Meshach, and Abednego, the three men who remained faithful to the true God, were made even more powerful in the government of Babylon.

The Writing on the Wall

WHEN Belshazzar was king of Babylon he gave a great party for his officers. There were more than a thousand officers at the party and they all drank a lot of wine.

While Belshazzar sipped his wine he said, "You know, I just remembered something."

"What is that?" some of the officers near him asked.

"I was just thinking about the war my father, Nebuchadnezzar, had with Israel. I remember that he brought back all the silver and gold cups he found in the Temple at Jerusalem. They are here in the palace! Why shouldn't we drink from silver and gold cups?"

"Great idea!" the officers agreed.

So the silver and gold cups from the Temple in Jerusalem were brought in and, of course, everyone thought they were splendid. The room buzzed with excitement.

"The Jews certainly had beautiful cups for their God," some soldiers said.

"Yes, they did. But our gods are more fun!"

"Yes—here's a toast to our gods with the God of Israel's cups!"

Everyone laughed and drank. But, suddenly, silence fell on the room. Belshazzar was staring at the wall in front of him.

The fingers of a human hand appeared on the wall, writing strange words! Belshazzar muttered the letters as they were written:

"M-E-N-E, M-E-N-E, T-E-K-E-L, U-P-H-A-R-S-I-N."

The writing stopped. The hand disappeared. Belshzzar shook with fright.

"Mene, Mene, Tekel, Upharsin," he said. "What do the words mean?"

But no one in the room could answer.

"Tell me what the words mean! Anyone who tells me what they mean will be rich and have the

MENE MENE TEKEL UPHARSIN

third place in my kingdom!"

The wisest men in Babylon went closer to the wall, but none of them could understand the words.

Belshazzar shook even more with fright. "Someone!" he shouted. "Someone tell me! What do the words mean?"

His mother heard him shouting and came into the hall.

"Don't be afraid," she said. "There is a man in Babylon who can tell you what the words mean. Your father brought him from Israel. He is a Jew and, now, the wisest man in Babylon."

"Who is he?"

"His name is Daniel."

"Bring Daniel here at once!" Belshazzar commanded his officers.

When Daniel was brought into the hall, the king asked, "Are you Daniel, the man my father brought from Israel?"

"Yes, I am."

"I want you to tell me what that writing on the wall means. If you can, I will give you great riches."

Daniel turned and read the words on the wall. Then he said:

"You can keep your riches. I will tell you what the words mean. Your father was a powerful king, Belshazzar. But he was proud and God punished him. For years your proud father ate grass like an animal in the fields—like a madman. That was God's punishment. You knew this, but you are proud, too—as proud as your father was. You have set yourself up against God. That is why God has sent this message."

"What does it mean?"

"'Mene' means that God has put a time limit on your reign. Your reign has ended. 'Tekel' means that God has weighed your actions and found them evil. 'Upharsin' means that your kingdom will be divided and given to the Medes and the Persians."

Belshazzar was not happy with the message, but he kept his promise and gave great riches to Daniel.

And everything happened as the writing on the wall had foretold. That night Belshazzar was murdered and Darius, the Mede, took over his kingdom.

Daniel in the Lions' Den

DARIUS the Mede was a very efficient king. When he took over the kingdom of Babylon, he divided it into small parts. Over each part he put a ruler, and then over these rulers he put three presidents. These presidents had the task of seeing that everything ran smoothly in the kingdom.

One of the three presidents was named Daniel. He was a Jew. He had come to Babylon years before as a captive. But he was very intelligent, and he was given important work in the governments of, first, King Nebuchadnezzar, then King Belshazzar, and now, King Darius.

Of the three presidents, Daniel was the best. In fact, he was so much better than the other two that King Darius thought about making him the only ruler of Babylon. Naturally, the other rulers of the kingdom were not happy about this. They held a meeting to talk about Daniel.

"We must find some way to get rid of Daniel," they agreed.

"Yes. Maybe we can find something that he has done wrong," one ruler suggested.

"No," another objected, "you can search until you're blue in the face. Daniel is very careful. He never does anything wrong."

"Yes, that's right," others agreed.

"He does have one weakness," one ruler said.

"What's that?"

"He's a Jew."

"What difference does that make?" all the other rulers objected. "Everyone knows he's a Jew."

"Yes, I know. But Jews worship only one God. Now, I have a plan. If we go about this carefully, we can get rid of Daniel forever."

"What's the plan?" everyone shouted.

The ruler explained his plan, and all the other rulers agreed that it was perfect.

"All right," the ruler said, "let's go and talk to King Darius."

So all of them went to the palace.

Darius received them kindly.

"What can I do for you today?" he said.

"O great king," one of the rulers said, "we have just had a long meeting and we feel there is a new law that you should make."

"Is that right?" the king said. "What is it?"

"We feel you should make a law that anyone who prays should pray only to you. They should not pray to anyone else—whether god or man. If they disobey, they should be thrown into the lions' den."

"You have thought about this matter for a long time?" the king asked.

"Yes, we have. We think it will be good for the kingdom. We think the law should be made to last for thirty days."

"Well—if you have discussed it, I suppose you are right. I will agree."

"Fine!" the ruler said. "But there is one more thing. We think you should make this law one that cannot be changed—not even by you."

"It is done!" the king said.

Word of the new law passed throughout the whole kingdom. Daniel, of course, heard about it, too. But he knew that there was only one true God and he continued to pray as he always had. Three times every day he knelt before the window in his room that faced Jerusalem and prayed to the true God.

The rulers were hoping he would do

this, and they had sent spies to watch Daniel. When the spies reported that Daniel was praying, the rulers went to King Darius immediately.

"O great king," they said, "didn't you make a law that no one could pray except to you, and that if a man prayed to anyone else he would be thrown into the lions' den?"

"Yes, I did. It is a law that cannot be changed."

"Well—Daniel continues to pray to the God of Israel! He is disobeying your law!"

The king was stunned. "Daniel? But..."

"O great king, Daniel disobeys the law!"

"Leave me alone," the king said. Darius did not want to put Daniel into the lions' den. He liked Daniel and he knew Daniel was a good ruler. All that day Darius thought and thought. How could he change the law? But he could not find a solution.

That evening, the rulers returned and said:

"O great king, the law cannot be changed. Daniel must be killed!"

Very sadly, the king answered, "Yes, I know. Leave me and send Daniel here."

When Daniel came, the king said, "Daniel, I have made a foolish law. But I cannot change it. I must put you in the lions' den."

Daniel did not speak.

"You have been faithful to your God," the king said. "Maybe He can save you."

And the king himself very sadly led Daniel to the lions' den and locked the door behind Daniel. Then the king returned to the palace. He could not eat and went to bed immediately. But he could not sleep, either. He tossed and turned on the bed all night. In the morning he ran to the lions' den and shouted:

"O Daniel! Daniel! Did your God save you?"

From behind the huge door came a faint voice.

"Don't worry, King Darius. My God sent an angel to save me. My God knows that I have never offended Him—nor you."

"Daniel's alive!" the king shouted with joy. "Open the door! Open the door! Let Daniel out!"

The guards opened the door and Daniel, unscratched, walked out. Darius could see the lions behind Daniel sitting quietly, content as kittens.

The king embraced Daniel and then shouted:

"Bring those rulers! Throw *them* to the lions!"

This was done, and the rulers were killed by the lions in an instant.

And Daniel, the faithful servant of the true God, became even more powerful in Babylon!

Queen Esther

AHASUERUS was a powerful king. His empire stretched from India in Asia to Ethiopia in Africa. But he was a lonely man. He had a beautiful wife at one time called Queen Vashti, but at a party he did something foolish. During the party he commanded Vashti to walk in front of the guests to show off her beauty. But Vashti refused, and Ahasuerus, in a fit of anger, had her banished from the empire. Now Ahasuerus was alone.

"We can solve your problem, King Ahasuerus," the king's servants said.

"How?"

"Why, we can go through the empire and find the most beautiful girls. Then you can choose the one you like for your wife."

"Do it!" Ahasuerus said. "I'm tired of being lonely."

Ahasuerus had an enormous palace and many people lived in it. One of these people was a Jew named Mordecai. He had been brought from Israel as a captive years before. Now he worked in the government. His cousin, Esther, lived with him. Esther's parents had died when she was young, and Mordecai treated her as his own daughter. She was very beautiful.

One day, the king's servants came to Esther and asked her to come to see the king. The moment Ahasuerus saw Esther he decided she would be his wife, the new queen of the empire. He treated her well and Esther was very happy.

Mordecai was very happy, too, until he heard one day that two men were planning to kill the king. He told this to Esther and she told her husband. Ahasuerus investigated the rumor and found it was true. The two men were caught and hanged. Nothing more was said about the matter—but everything was written down in the king's history book.

Some time later Ahasuerus named a man called Haman to be the head of his government. He gave Haman great power and commanded all the people to bow whenever Haman passed by.

Haman was very proud of himself. Everywhere he went people bowed down to him as if he were a god. But then he began to notice that one man always refused to bow.

"Who is that man?" he asked his guards angrily.

"He is called Mordecai," they answered.

"Why does he not bow like the others?"

"He is a Jew."

"What? The law makes no exceptions for Jews!"

"Jews bow only to their God."

"Is that right? Well—we'll see about that!"

Haman was so angry that he decided he would have all the Jews in the empire killed. He went to the king.

"King Ahasuerus," he said, "there is a group of people in the empire that are dangerous. They have their own laws and do not obey ours! I think they should all be killed. If you sign a law to have them killed, I will give $20,000,000 of my own money to pay the expenses."

"Keep the money, Haman," Ahasuerus answered. "Do whatever you want. If these people are dangerous, they should be gotten rid of."

And Haman put out a law that all Jews should be killed.

When Mordecai heard what had happened, he put on rough clothes and sprinkled ashes on his head. This is what Jews do at times of great sadness. All the other Jews in the empire did the same thing.

When Esther heard how

Mordecai was dressed she sent her maid with new clothes for him, but he refused to wear them.

"Why won't he wear the new clothes?" Esther asked her maid.

"He says that there is a new law that all Jews must be killed. Here—look. This is a copy of the law that he gave me."

"This is terrible!"

"He wants you to go to the king and make him change his mind."

"Go to the king! But Mordecai knows I can't do that! No one can go to the king unless the king calls him. Death is the penalty! The king hasn't called me for thirty days. Mordecai knows that."

"But if the king points his golden scepter at you, you will not be killed."

"Yes. But how can I be sure he will do that? Go tell Mordecai I can't do it."

When Mordecai heard the message he sent a reply to Esther:

"Have you forgotten you are a Jew? Do you think Haman will kill all the Jews and spare you because you are queen? No, you must see the king. Perhaps God has made you queen so that you might save your people."

When Esther heard Mordecai's reply, she said to her maid:

"He is right. I must defend my people. Tell Mordecai that all Jews must pray and fast for me. If I die, I will die. But I will see the king!"

But there was nothing for Esther to fear after all. When she approached the king, he pointed his golden scepter at her and smiled.

"What do you wish, my queen?"

"I have prepared a feast for today, my lord. Would you and Haman come?"

"Why, certainly," the king answered.

Haman was enormously pleased.

He went to the feast that night and later told his wife:

"I'm becoming more famous every day! Just think of it! The queen makes a feast just for the king and *me*!"

"But why?" his wife said. "The queen must want something from the king."

"Yes, I think so. Even the king asked her what she wanted."

"And?"

"And we're invited to another feast tomorrow! The queen said she will tell us tomorrow."

"My! The queen must see how important you are!"

"Yes! Yes! What a wonderful day! Except for one thing."

"What is that?"

"Oh, it's that Mordecai. I passed him again on the way home. He still won't bow down to me. He makes me furious."

"Well, there's a way to stop that," he wife reminded him.

"Yes, I know. But it will take time to arrange to have all the Jews killed. Meanwhile, I still have to pass that man."

"Why wait? Build a gallows and have Mordecai hanged at once."

"Yes! Yes, you're right. I'll ask the king to give the order right away. I'll have the soldiers build the gallows tonight, and tomorrow, after the feast, we'll hang Mordecai!"

That same night the king could not sleep, so he sat up and began to read his history book. He happened to open the book at the page that told the story of how Mordecai saved the king from being killed by two men. Ahasuerus called his servant.

"This man Mordecai, did we ever do anything for him? He saved my life."

"No, sir, nothing was done."

"Hmmm. Is there anyone in the palace who can carry out an order for me?"

"Haman just arrived, sir. He wanted to see you."

"Send him in."

Haman entered and said, "King Ahasuerus, I have a request."

"It'll have to wait, Haman. I have a question for you. What if you knew a man who did a great thing for me? What should I do for him?"

Haman thought to himself, "He must mean *me*." He answered the king:

"Why, I think you should clothe him in your own robes, give him your horse, and put a crown on his head. Then have him led throughout the city and have an important official walk beside him and say, 'This is how the king treats a man who is worthy of honor.'"

"Very good, Haman. We will do it that way. You take care of everything."

"You did not say who the man was, King Ahasuerus."

"Oh, of course. His name is Mordecai."

"Morde. . .!"

"Yes, Hurry! Do everything just the way you told me."

And Haman was forced to put the king's robes and a crown on Mordecai and lead him through the streets on the king's horse and shout, "This is how the king treats a man who is worthy of honor."

When Haman had finished he went home.

"How embarrassing!" he said to his wife. "To have to lead the man I hate most through the city streets!"

"This looks bad for you, Haman," his wife said. "But don't worry. The gallows are ready. You can hang Mordecai after the feast."

"I don't know," Haman said worriedly. "I don't know."

At the feast, the king said to Esther:

"This is the second feast you have made for Haman and myself, Queen Esther. Now, what is it you really want? I will give you anything."

"I would like you to save my life," Esther said, "and the lives of my people."

"Your life? What do you mean?"

"I and my people, the Jews, have been condemned to death."

"Who gave such an order? Who would dare do such a thing?"

"Why—it is this wretch, Haman." Haman's face turned white.

"Haman?" the king shouted in rage. "What kind of business is this? You told me you were going to kill my enemies. You didn't tell me you meant the Jews!"

"I...I..." Haman stuttered.

"Guard!" the king shouted. "This man is condemned to death!"

"How convenient," the guard said. "There is a gallows built outside Haman's door. Haman was going to hang Mordecai on it."

"Mordecai! The man who saved my life?"

"Yes."

"Hang Haman on it!"

And so the Jews were saved!

Jews today still celebrate that great day when they were saved by Queen Esther. They call it the day of Purim.

NEW TESTAMENT

The First Christmas

ABOUT two thousand years ago a Roman emperor named Augustus ruled a large part of the world. His empire was so large, in fact, he did not know how many people were in it. So he decided to have the people counted.

"I want a census of the whole Roman Empire," he said to his attendants.

"That will not be easy, sir."

"I know. But I must know how many people there are in the empire. You will tell everyone to return to their home town. It will be easier to count them that way."

"Yes, sir."

Many, many miles away in Israel there lived two people for whom Augustus's order was very hard. Joseph and Mary were married and Mary was going to have a baby very soon. They lived in Nazareth, where Joseph worked as a carpenter. But now, because of the census, they would have to travel all the way to Bethlehem. Bethlehem was Joseph's home town.

So one day they set out. They walked for four days up and down the hills until, finally, from the top of one hill they could look down and see Bethlehem.

Bethlehem was crowded. Everyone had come home to be counted. The streets were filled with people—people with wagons, people with bundles of clothes on their backs; some shouting happily to each other, others grumbling because of all the trouble Augustus was causing.

"Well, hello, Eli! Haven't seen you in years! How's the family?" one would say.

"Who does this emperor think he is, anyway?" another would grumble. "I know why he wants this census. He wants to tax us all! That's why!"

Joseph and Mary passed through the crowd toward the inn. Joseph knew that Mary would have her baby soon and he wanted to find a comfortable spot for her.

The inn of Bethlehem was not a large, warm house, but in those days it was considered comfortable. It was nothing more than a large square of ground surrounded by four walls, with an opening in the front wall that served as a door. There was no roof over the inn, but along the walls there were covered platforms where people could sleep without getting wet. Their animals slept on the ground in the middle.

Joseph went to the door of the inn. The inn was packed with people and animals!

"Don't tell me you hope to get in here," someone said to Joseph.

"Yes. My wife is going to have a baby," Joseph answered.

"Well—take a look for yourself. The people are practically on top of each other. I don't think this would be a good spot for your wife. There's just no room!"

"Yes, I see. You're right. I'll have to find someplace else."

"Why not try those caves up in the hills? They're not too beautiful, but you'll have a roof over your head. There's no more room around here."

"Yes. Thank you."

And so Joseph and Mary walked up to the hills and found a cave. There were some sheep and oxen in the cave and a manger with straw in it.

And that night Mary had her baby, the most beautiful baby ever born. His name was Jesus.

The Shepherds

I WISH there was more grass in this country," a shepherd named Benjamin said to his companions. They were sitting on a hill near Bethlehem, watching their sheep. It was a clear, starlit night.

"Ha! More grass! How could this desert ever give you more grass?"

"Oh, I know," Benjamin answered. "I guess I'm just tired of following these sheep around day and night looking for food."

"That's a shepherd's life."

"I guess so."

"Oh, cheer up, man! It's not a bad life."

"I'm not so sure. These people think we're funny."

"Funny?"

"Yes! They think we're all no good. They think we're thieves!"

"Well, Benjamin, some shepherds . . ."

"I know, I know! But that doesn't mean we're all bad. Why, last month, my cousin Micah's cow was stolen and I went to court to tell the judge that I knew the man who stole it. Do you know what the judge said?"

"What?"

"He said: 'You're a shepherd. No one can trust a shepherd's word. Your word is no good in this court.' That's what he said, sure as I'm standing here."

"Oh—people just don't understand."

"Don't understand! Why don't they remember that David was a shepherd? David! The greatest king Israel ever had! David was a shepherd! Right here in these fields!"

"Come on, now, Benjamin. Stop that talk! There's nothing you can do about it. Relax. It's a lovely night."

"I'm cold. I . . ."

The shepherd stopped talking suddenly. A blazing light, brighter than lightning, lit up the hill before them.

"What—what is . . ." the shepherds shouted in fright.

Then in the middle of the light an angel appeared.

"Do not be afraid," he said. "Behold, I bring you good tidings of great joy. I bring you wonderful news!"

The shepherds huddled together, still a bit afraid. They had never seen anything like this before.

"Listen," the angel continued. "Today, in Bethlehem, the city of David, your Saviour was born. Christ, the Lord, was born today! This is how you will find him. Look for a baby wrapped in white cloths and lying in a manger. That baby is the Saviour!"

And then an army of angels appeared, all saying:

"Glory to God in the highest, and on earth peace, good will toward men."

Then, just as suddenly as they had come, the angels disappeared. The shepherds stared at each other, trying to talk.

"It . . . it . . ."

"Angels . . . the angels . . ."

"We must . . . I . . ."

"Come! What a wonderful . . .

Come! We must find the baby!"

"But where?"

"In a manger. The angel said he was lying in a manger. He must be in one of the caves!"

So the shepherds ran off toward the caves. They looked into one cave after another. Then they found the right one. They saw Mary and Joseph, and cows and oxen and sheep warming the cave with their breath. And there, in the center, they saw a manger, and in the manger, a tiny baby wrapped in white cloths.

"It is he!"

"The angels sent us," the shepherds said to Mary and Joseph. "They said we would find the Saviour of the world here!"

Mary and Joseph only nodded and smiled.

The shepherds did not know what to do. They shuffled their feet. They bowed. They knelt down. Never had they known such joy.

"And to think—God called us first. Shepherds!"

"What do you think of a shepherd's life now, Benjamin?"

Benjamin could hardly talk. "People forget us," he said. "But—but God remembers."

The Glory of the People

"I GET discouraged sometimes, Anna," Simeon said. He was at the door of the Temple in Jerusalem. "I'm getting very old."

"No older than I, Simeon," Anna answered.

"I know. But I feel my end is near. This old body won't last much longer. I come to the Temple every day, expecting to see the Saviour. But every day it is the same. He does not come. How many days do I have left?"

"God has promised that you will see the Saviour before you die. You must not be discouraged. God always keeps His word. Look at me. Ever since my husband died I have lived here in the Temple—waiting for the Saviour. I'm not discouraged."

"You are a good woman, Anna."

"And you are a good man. Now, put a smile on your face. The Saviour will come."

"I know. I must be more patient."

"We must leave Bethlehem and go to Jerusalem," Joseph said to Mary. "Jesus will be eight days old tomorrow. We must bring him to the Temple to present him to God."

"But what will we bring for a sacrifice?" Mary asked. "We cannot afford a lamb."

"I will buy two perfect doves at the Temple door. They are a poor man's offering. But God understands."

So, the next day, Joseph and Mary walked to Jerusalem. Joseph bought the doves for a few pennies. Then they started to enter the Temple. Mary carried the baby Jesus.

But Simeon stopped them at the door. He knew now that the Saviour had finally come. He took Jesus in his arms and said:

"Now, my dear God, I can die in peace—just as You promised. I have seen him! He is the light of the world. He is the glory of the people of Israel!"

Joseph and Mary looked at each other, amazed that Simeon could know such things.

Simeon then said to Mary, "Your child will be rejected by many in Israel and this will give you great sorrow. Your sorrow will be like a sword through your heart. But he will bring great happiness to many, also."

As Simeon spoke, Anna walked nearer.

"He has come!" she said. "The Saviour of the world is here!"

And she ran off, telling everyone she could find that the Saviour had finally come.

Then Mary and Joseph took Jesus and offered him to God. Never had the Temple in Jerusalem known such glory!

They walked back to Bethlehem quietly, thinking over what they had heard. They thought about the sorrow Jesus would have—and Mary held him closer. But they also thought about the happiness that Jesus would bring to so many people. This tiny baby in Mary's arms was the Saviour. He was the light of the world! He was the glory of the people!

The Wise Men

THERE are three men waiting to see you, King Herod," the servant said. Herod was king of the Jews at the time Jesus was born. The Romans were the true rulers of the country, but they let Herod continue as king.

"What do they want?" Herod asked.

"I'm not sure, my lord. They came from the east and I cannot understand them too well. I think they are looking for the king of the Jews."

"I am king of the Jews!"

"Yes, my lord. But I don't think that is what they mean. I . . ."

"Agh! Stop mumbling like a fool. You never get anything straight! Let them in!"

The servant slunk nervously toward the door. He opened it and said:

"King Herod will see you now."

The three men walked in. They were all dressed in rich robes. When Herod saw how rich the men looked, his face brightened.

"Come in! Come in, my dear sirs!" he said in his most oily manner. "What can I do for you?"

"King Herod," one of the wise men said, "please accept our apologies. We know you are a busy man . . ."

"No—no! No bother at all. It is a pleasure to meet you."

"Why—thank you. We are three wise men from the east. We have come in search of the king of the Jews."

"Well, your search is ended. I am king of the Jews."

"Ah—yes, King Herod, we know that. But we are referring to the king that has just been born; the king that was foretold many, many years ago."

"Foretold? But—but how do

156

you know he was just born?"

"We followed a star—a very bright star. It led us here to Jerusalem. But then the star disappeared."

Herod was silent. This talk of a new king disturbed him.

"Well," Herod said, "what do you want me to do?"

"King Herod, is there no one in your palace who could tell us where the king was born?"

"Ah—well, I'll see." Herod turned to his servant. "Send some of the religious leaders here."

The religious leaders came in a short time.

"Sirs," Herod said, "these wise men are searching for the new king of the Jews—I think they must mean the Messiah. Do you know where the Messiah is to be born?"

"King Herod, we know whom these men are looking for. All of Jerusalem is buzzing with rumors about the new king."

"All of Jerusalem?" Herod said worriedly.

"Yes. So we have prepared ourselves. We have studied the scriptures and have found what the prophet Micah foretold about the Messiah. Look."

They showed the scriptures to Herod. He read:

"Bethlehem, you are not an unimportant town—for in you will be born the leader of the people of Israel."

"The king must be in Bethlehem!" the wise men said.

"Yes," Herod said politely. He was in a rage, but he hid his rage and spoke with a very kind voice. "Now you must go and find the child. But—I ask one favor of you."

"Yes?"

"When you find him, come back and tell me where he is. I wish to go and worship him, too!"

"Definitely, King Herod."

And the wise men left the palace and started toward Bethlehem. They had not gone very far when they looked up.

"Look! Look! The star has appeared again!"

Once more they followed the star, and it led them to the very place where Jesus was. They went into the house and gave Jesus presents of gold, frankincense, and myrrh. They had found the king of the Jews!

But that night, God appeared to them in a dream and warned them that Herod wanted to harm the child. So they went home another way—and avoided Herod completely.

157

To Egypt

I WONDER what is keeping those wise men?" Herod said to his servant. "They were supposed to return and tell me where that new king is."

"I haven't heard any word, my lord," the servant said.

"You never hear anything, you fool! Well, I've waited long enough. They can't stay in Bethlehem forever. You go down to Bethlehem and find out where they are."

"Yes, my lord."

When the servant had left, Herod thought to himself, "I must do something about this new king. I know my people. They'll start rumors that the Messiah has come. Then they'll want to make him king in my place. And that'll be the end of me! No—I have to do something!"

The servant returned that same evening. He tapped nervously on King Herod's door.

"Who is it?" Herod called.

"Your servant, my lord. I am back."

"Well, come in and stop talking through the door!"

The servant entered slowly. He closed the door with great care, then turned and faced Herod. He wrung his hands fearfully.

"What's the matter with you?" Herod said impatiently. "Come over here and tell me what you found out."

"Ah—sir—my lord . . ."

"My lord—my majesty! Will you stop wasting my time! Tell me. Out with it! Did you go to Bethlehem?"

"Yes, my . . . yes, I did."

"And?"

"And—"

"Agh! Did you see the wise men?"

"Yes, er, no, my lord."

"No? Why not?"

"They are not in Bethlehem."

"They must be on their way to Jerusalem."

"No, er, sir."

"No?"

The servant cringed back toward the door.

"Where are they, then?" Herod shouted. "They said they would come back."

"They left . . . left Bethlehem by another road. They are not coming to Jerusalem."

"Then where are they?" Herod was red with anger.

"I don't know."

"Don't know! Don't know! Tell me this—did you look for the child? Did you find out what house the wise men went into?"

"No, my lord."

"Why not?"

"I didn't know I was supposed . . ."

"Good-for-nothing! Get out! Get out! I'll decide tomorrow what I must do. Out!"

That same night, an angel appeared to Joseph.

"Get up, Joseph," the angel said.

"Wha . . . ?" Joseph muttered, trying to stir himself.

"Get up. Take the child and his mother to Egypt."

"To Egypt?"

"Yes. Herod wishes to kill the child. You will be safe in Egypt."

"I will get ready."

"I will tell you when it is safe to return to this country." The angel then disappeared.

Joseph shook his wife. "Mary! Come—we must leave immediately. Herod wants to kill Jesus. You get the boy ready. I'll pack our things and get the donkey."

Within the hour they were on their way to Egypt. Mary, with Jesus in her arms, rode on the donkey and Joseph walked beside them. No one noticed them leaving because it was still night and everyone was still asleep.

The next morning, Herod called his guard.

"I have a difficult job for you—but you must be loyal to me. It is your duty."

"Anything, sir," the guard answered.

"There is a child in Bethlehem whom the people are trying to make king. The Romans won't stand for this. You know how they control this country and they don't like fake kings. I am king. The Romans have said so."

"There is no doubt about that, sir. What do you want me to do?"

"I've been thinking. Those wise men couldn't have seen that star too long ago. I think they even mentioned two years. So this child cannot be more than two years old."

"Yes, sir?"

"Now, listen carefully. I want you to take some soldiers and go to Bethlehem."

"Immediately, sir!"

"And kill every baby boy under two years of age!"

"Kill . . . ?" The guard was startled.

"Yes, kill them!"

"But, sir . . . so young . . . "

"Do it! Now! Or I will have your life!"

"Yes, sir," the guard said sorrowfully.

And the soldiers did as Herod commanded them. Every boy baby under two in Bethlehem was killed. In the city all that could be heard was screaming and weeping.

Sometime later the terrible Herod died. The angel appeared to Joseph again.

"It is safe to return now," he said. So Joseph took Mary and Jesus and returned to Israel. They settled in a town called Nazareth.

Jesus Lost

WHEN Jesus was twelve years old, his parents said to him:

"Jesus, we must make a journey to Jerusalem. We must go to the Temple for the feast. Now, you are only twelve years old and the law of God does not oblige you to go. But we think it will be good for you."

How wonderful! Jerusalem! And the Temple!

The next week they began the trip—Joseph and Mary and Jesus. It was not a very long journey, but because of the great crowds of people on the road, all going to Jerusalem for the feast, the journey took four days.

But what a wonderful journey—filled with such great memories. They passed Mount Tabor and then Gilboa, where King Saul and his son Jonathan died. Off in the distance they could see Mount Carmel, where Elijah defied the priests of Baal. Later, they passed Dothan, where Jacob's son, Joseph, had been thrown in the well by his brothers. Finally, on the last day, they saw the high towers and walls of Jerusalem itself!

Joseph and Mary did not spend many days in Jerusalem. They had to get back to their work in Nazareth. And so, after they had worshiped in the Temple and celebrated the feast, they started back with a large crowd of people.

"Joseph," Mary asked suddenly, "have you seen Jesus?"

"He must be with some of our relatives," Joseph answered. "Let him be. He will enjoy himself with the other children. I'll find him tonight. Come along."

Mary and Joseph walked for a whole day. They were not worried about Jesus. All the children gathered together in the crowd. Nothing was unusual.

Jesus would be at supper with them that evening.

But evening came and Jesus did not appear. All the other children were eating with their parents, but Jesus was nowhere in sight.

Joseph and Mary went from tent to tent, asking for Jesus. But no one had seen him.

"No, he wasn't playing with us today," the children said.

"Come, Mary," Joseph said. "We must return to Jerusalem."

When they got back to the city, Joseph and Mary searched everywhere for Jesus. For three whole days they went from house to house. But no one had seen Jesus.

Finally, in despair, they went to the Temple to pray to God for help. And there—to their surprise—they found Jesus. He was sitting in the center of a circle of very learned men, asking and answering questions.

"Jesus!" Mary murmured in relief.

A man passing nearby said: "Do you know that boy?"

"He is my son," Mary answered.

"An amazing boy, your son. I've never known of anyone so young to be so wise. An amazing boy!"

At that, Jesus looked up and saw his parents. He ran to them and hugged them.

"Jesus," Mary said, "do you know how worried your father and I have been? We've been looking for you for days."

"But I did not want to cause you sorrow, mother. You should have known I was here. I must do my Father's business."

Mary and Joseph did not understand what Jesus meant. But they forgot their sorrow soon enough. Jesus returned to Nazareth with them and brought his parents joy every day. He grew into a strong young man.

And everyone loved him, both God and man.

Come, Follow Me

JESUS spent many years in Nazareth with Mary and Joseph. He did ordinary things, worked at an ordinary job, and people must have thought he was a very ordinary person. After all, no one from Nazareth had ever done anything very famous. But Jesus knew better. He knew he had been sent by God, his Father, to change the world, to save men from their sins. When he was about thirty years old, he knew it was time to begin his work.

He began by talking to the people about God. The people were astounded. They had never heard anyone who could talk like this! And little by little, more people came to hear Jesus' words.

One day, Jesus was standing on the shore of the Sea of Galilee. He began talking and the crowd of people became so large that they almost pushed Jesus into the water.

Jesus turned toward the water and saw two boats. The fishermen had just finished their work and were cleaning and drying their nets.

"Simon," Jesus said.

"Yes?" one of the fishermen answered, astounded that Jesus should know his name.

"I would like to use your boat. There is no room left here along the shore."

"Why—certainly. Here—let me help you get in."

Jesus stepped into the boat. "Now," he said, "pull out a bit from shore."

Simon did as he was told. And Jesus sat on the bow of the boat and spoke to the people from there.

It was a beautiful day. The sun danced on the water and birds sang. The people stood and listened, amazed at the things Jesus told them.

Jesus spoke for a long while. At last he sent the people to their homes. Then he turned to Simon.

"Thank you for letting me use your boat."

"Very happy . . . er, I'm glad . . ." Simon stumbled over his words. He was a big, strong man, but he felt like a boy in front of this astounding man. He wiped his hands on his robe and tried to think of something to say.

"Now," Jesus said, "call Andrew, your brother, and take both boats out into the deep water. We are going fishing!"

Simon scratched his head. Jesus, obviously, was a very wise man. But Simon had been a fisherman all his life. He had been fishing all night with Andrew and they had caught nothing. It was no use trying again. A fisherman must be patient. Tomorrow would be another day.

But there was something in the way Jesus spoke—kindly, yet very strong. It was difficult to say "no" to Jesus.

"Well, Master," Simon said, "we have fished all night and caught nothing. But, if you say so, we'll try again. We'll put the nets back into the water."

Jesus nodded.

"Andrew!" Simon called. "Get your nets ready! We're going out again!"

"Wha . . . ?" Andrew called back.

"Never mind! Just come! Hurry!"

And the two boats moved out, side by side, to the deep water.

"Here," Jesus said. "Put your nets down here."

Andrew looked over at his

brother. He wondered why they were doing such a silly thing. But, shrugging his shoulders, he tossed the net over the side of the boat.

They sat there a while. Nothing seemed to be happening.

"Well," Simon thought to himself, "it's no surprise. Jesus is a land person. He doesn't know much about fishing."

But then, slowly, the boats began to lean to the side with the weight of the nets.

"Simon!" Andrew called. "SIMON! The nets! The nets! I can't move mine!"

Simon pulled at his nets. "Fish!" he shouted. "Lots of fish!"

"My nets are going to break, Simon! They won't hold."

"Help!" Simon yelled. "We need help!" He looked toward the shore. He saw other fishermen there. Two of them were his friends. "Ahoy! James! John! Help!"

On the shore, James and John held their hands to their ears, as if to hear better.

"Help!" Andrew shouted. "Come! Quick! Fish! Help!"

James and John held up their arms. They couldn't understand. Simon and Andrew began waving their arms frantically.

"Fish! Come!"

Finally, James and John understood. They climbed into their boat and came toward Simon and Andrew.

"What's the matter?" they called when they were closer.

"The nets are breaking!"

"You've got fish?"

"Yes! A catch like you never saw!"

John and James drew their boat closer. They jumped over into Simon's boat. All together, the men pulled, and sweated, and grunted. Finally, they got the fish on board. And both Simon's and Andrew's boats almost began to sink with the weight of the fish. Slowly, they brought the boats back to shore.

Simon shook his head. "It's not possible," he thought. Then he turned to Jesus. "Lord," he said. "I am a sinful man. Leave me."

"Do not worry," Jesus said. "From now on all of you will be fishers of men. Simon, your new name is Peter. Now, all of you— Peter, Andrew, James, John— come, follow me."

And all of them left everything and followed Jesus. Later, others would join them—twelve men in all. In the future they would be known as apostles.

A Wedding at Cana

WEDDINGS are always happy events. People gather together and dance and celebrate the beginning of a new family. But, in the days of Jesus, weddings were reason for even greater celebration. Not only did the family and a few friends celebrate—the whole town joined in!

That is why, that week, the whole town of Cana was full of laughter and singing. There was going to be a wedding. People ran back and forth decorating homes, strewing the streets with flowers and ribbons.

Mary, Jesus' mother, was there, too. And she worked as hard as anyone else—and sang just as happily.

A wedding!

A tent was put up in the middle of the town. The ceremony would take place there. A short distance away, two thrones were placed on a high platform. The new husband and wife would sit on the thrones like king and queen and all the people would pass by, honoring the new couple on their great day.

"Mary!" a woman called. "Help me with these flowers, please. I can't get them to sit right around the throne."

"Certainly!" Mary ran to help.

"Is Jesus coming to the wedding?"

"I'm not sure," Mary said. "I hope so. I know he must do his Father's work. But he would enjoy this! He loves to see people happy!"

On Tuesday evening, the ceremony began. Relatives prepared the bride. They dressed her in the most lovely gown possible, put a crown on her head, rings on her fingers, and bracelets on her wrists and

170

ankles.

In his home, the groom put on his finest robe. Then the procession began. All the towns-people gathered together. They all had torches in their hands. Some carried tambourines and flutes. Singing and cheering, they led the groom to the bride's house—and from there to the tent, where the couple became husband and wife.

Then the party began! It would last for two or three days!

On the second day, Jesus and his disciples arrived. Mary spotted him.

"Oh, Jesus, I'm so glad you could come!"

"I did not want to miss it."

"Well, enjoy yourself. But—but there's just one thing . . ."

"Yes?"

"I just noticed that the wine is running out. More people came than expected. The bride and groom are very embarrassed."

"But what can I do about that?"

The servants did as they were told. They filled the jars to the top.

"Now," Jesus said, "take out a cupful and bring it to the wine steward."

They did as he said and ran to the wine steward. He drank from the cup.

"Why!" he said, "this is the most splendid wine I've ever tasted."

The wine steward went to the bridegroom.

"Sir," he said, "this is the strangest wedding I've ever been to. Most times, the bridegroom serves the best wine first and then, when the people have drunk for a while, he serves the poorer wine. But you—you have kept the best wine of all for last. I don't understand."

But the bridegroom could not answer. He did not know what had happened either. He just smiled and returned to the celebration.

The celebration continued and Jesus happily joined in. His disciples, however, saw what he had done and they were astounded. Their faith in Jesus grew.

Afterwards, many said that it was the best wedding they had ever attended.

Mary smiled and ran off to see the people who were taking care of the wine.

"Oh, Mary," the wine steward said, "this is terrible! How embarrassing! There is no more wine! What are we going to do?"

"Send some servants to Jesus," Mary answered, "and tell them to do whatever he says."

The servants went to Jesus.

"There are six stone jars standing there," Jesus said. "They hold about twenty gallons. Fill them with water."

The Well at Sychar

ONE day Jesus was walking with his disciples through the country of Samaria. At about noon they came to a well that many years before Jacob had given to his son, Joseph. It was called the well at Sychar. Jesus was tired and he sat down beside the well.

"It is good that you rest," Peter said. "You stay here and we will go into the town to get some food."

When the disciples had gone, a woman came to the well to draw out some water.

"Give me a drink, please," Jesus asked her.

"What?" She was astounded. In those days, Jews did not talk to Samaritans. They were enemies. "You are a Jew, sir. How is it that you ask me, a Samaritan, for a drink?"

"If you only knew," Jesus replied, "what God is offering you, and who it is who asked you for a drink, you would have asked me for a drink of living water."

The woman was confused. "But—you don't have a bucket, sir."

"No."

"This well is very deep. How could you get the water—this *living* water you talk about? Are you a greater man than Jacob who gave us this well?"

Jesus answered, "Anyone who drinks the water from this well will soon be thirsty again. But anyone who drinks the water that I give will never be thirsty again. The water will become like a well inside him. It will give him eternal life."

The woman was still confused. She was still not sure what Jesus was talking about. But she was a practical woman, so she said:

"Sir, give me some of that water. That way I won't ever be

thirsty again and I won't have to come back here to draw water ever again."

"Go, call your husband," Jesus said, "and bring him here."

"I don't have a husband."

"That's true," Jesus said. "You have had five husbands and the one you have now is not your true husband."

"Er . . ." The woman was certainly confused now. She tried to change the subject:

"Sir, I see you are a prophet. You know all kinds of things. Now, tell me, our ancestors always worshiped on this mountain, but you Jews say that Jerusalem is where everyone should worship. What do you think about that?"

"Believe me, the time is coming when you will worship the Father neither on this mountain, nor in Jerusalem."

"Oh?"

"True worshipers will worship God in their hearts. That is what the Father wants."

"Well—er—I know the Messiah is coming and he will tell us everything."

"I am the Messiah!"

The woman drew in her breath. But before she could speak, the disciples returned. The woman got up and ran back to town.

"Master," the disciples said, "take something to eat. You must be hungry."

"I have food that you know nothing about."

The disciples looked at each other. "Did someone bring you food?" one asked.

"Doing my Father's work is my food. Look at the fields—the wheat is heavy and leaning over.

It is time for the harvest. I must complete my Father's work; I must bring in His harvest. And you must help me."

As he was saying this, a large crowd of Samaritans came toward the well, led by the woman who had talked with Jesus.

"Sir," a man said, "this woman says you are the Messiah, that you told her everything about her private life. We would like to hear you speak."

And Jesus spoke to them for a long while. When he had finished, the Samaritans said to the woman:

"Now we believe—not because you told us—but because we have heard him with our own ears. We know he is the Saviour of the world."

Peter's Mother-in-Law

ONE day, Jesus was teaching in the synagogue in the town of Capernaum. There was a man listening to him who had a devil in him.

The devil began to shout:

"Agh! Jesus! What are you doing here? Don't bother us!"

Jesus stopped teaching.

"You want to destroy us!" the voice continued.

The people in the synagogue became very disturbed.

"I know who you are," the voice screamed. "You are the holy one of God!"

"Quiet!" Jesus said in a strong voice. "Come out of that man, and leave him alone!"

And the devil threw the man down to the floor and came out of him. Jesus went to the man and helped him up. He was not hurt.

As Jesus came out of the synagogue, several disciples came up to him.

"Master, Peter's mother-in-law is quite sick. He would like you to come down to see her."

"We'll go right away."

They walked to the house, and when they arrived they saw the worried look on all the relatives' faces.

"Master," Peter said, "thank you for coming. She is very sick. A very high fever has taken hold of her."

"Show me where she is," Jesus said.

The poor woman was moaning in the bed.

Jesus went directly to her. He leaned over the bed and said:

"Fever! Do not torture this woman! Leave her in peace!"

And, immediately, the fever left and Peter's mother-in-law jumped up, healthier than she had ever been! She recovered so well that she began to get supper ready for everyone in the house!

The Tempest

THE fame of Jesus' power attracted many, many people. Some came for cure of a sickness, others came to hear him talk, and others were just curious. For whatever reason, they were always around him and it was difficult for Jesus to get any rest.

So, one day, he decided to cross the large lake, called the Sea of Galilee, with his disciples. When he got into the boat, he went to the back and lay down and fell asleep immediately.

The boat left the shore. All the disciples were happy. This was a nice rest for them all. The weather was fine, and several of them were fisherman, so they had no fear of the water.

But the Sea of Galilee is treacherous! It can change from a calm lake to a raging sea in a few minutes.

When they were about in the middle of the lake, Peter said:

"The wind has changed. We may have some trouble."

And sure enough, in a short while the wind grew stronger and tiny white waves began to build on the water. Then the sky grew darker, and the boat began to bob on larger waves.

"Storm's coming!" Peter shouted.

"Should we wake Jesus?" another disciple asked.

"No—let him sleep," Peter answered. "I've made it through plenty of storms."

But the sky grew darker yet and the waves rose high enough to lash water into the boat. Then the rain hit, heavy sheets splashing down on them. The boat bounced like a puppet dangling on strings.

"Bail that water out!" Peter shouted. "Hurry! This is bad!"

The boat lurched toward the sky, then dove down again, then lurched to the side. Huge waves

180

poured into the boat.

"We're sinking!"

Peter ran to Jesus. "Master! Master! Wake up! We're sinking!"

Jesus woke up calmly and looked at the disciples.

"Why are you afraid?"

"We're sinking! We're lost!"

"How little faith you have." Jesus stood up and held his hands out over the sea.

"Be still!" he commanded. "Be calm!"

And immediately the lake settled down and the surface became like a sheet of glass.

The disciples looked at each other.

"What kind of power is this?" they asked. "Even the sea and the wind obey him."

The Pool

IN JERUSALEM there is a pool called the Sheep Pool, or the Pool of Bethesda. It was a famous pool. It had walls built all around it and. a roof jutted out from the walls.

All manner of sick people stayed under this roof. They were waiting for the water in the pool to move.

"Do you really believe the story about the water?" one sick man said to another.

"What do you mean? Believe?"

"Do you really think an angel comes down and touches the water, and that the first one into the water after the angel comes will be cured of any sickness?"

"Look—I've been here for months. I've seen it happen. Of course, I believe."

"Why aren't you cured, then?"

"I'm too weak. Someone always gets to the water before me. But—but I'll make it someday."

"Ha! Good luck!"

"I've had this sickness thirty-eight years. But my day will come."

While the man was talking, Jesus came into the pool. He walked directly to the man.

"Do you want to be well again?" Jesus asked.

"Do I?" the man said. "Of course I do. But I don't have anyone to help me to the water. Someone always gets there before me. Will you help me the next time the water moves?"

"Get up," Jesus said quietly.

"Wha—? But I . . . I . . . "

"Get up, pick up your blanket, and walk."

The man stood up. His legs were strong under him!

"I'm well," he shouted, and he ran off with his blanket. As he came out of the pool he ran into some men.

"Hey!" they shouted. "Hold on, there! Don't you know it's

the Sabbath? You're old enough to know the law."

"Of course I know. I . . . "

"Then why are you carrying your blanket? You know it is against the law to carry a blanket on the Sabbath."

"Why—the man who cured me told me to pick up my blanket and walk."

"Who cured you? Who told you to carry your blanket?"

"Who? He . . . I don't know. He's right in the pool here. Come, look!"

They walked into the pool.

"There!" the man said. "No! No—that's not him. There! No. No—I can't see him in this crowd."

"A likely story. You people will invent any story to break the Sabbath."

"But it's true! It's true, I tell you."

"It's bad enough breaking the Sabbath. Don't become a liar, too."

"But—but he came to me right over . . . "

The men turned and walked away. The cured man just stood there—completely flustered. Then he looked down at his legs and remembered: "I'm cured!" He dropped his blanket and ran off.

Some time later Jesus saw the man in the Temple and spoke to him again:

"You are well again now. Don't sin any more, or something worse might happen to you."

"Yes, sir."

Jesus turned to walk away.

"Sir?" the man called.

"Yes?"

"What is your name?"

"I am called Jesus of Nazareth."

As soon as Jesus left, the man ran to find those who had stopped him. He found them outside the Temple.

"Listen!" he said. "It's true! Everything I told you is true. You can ask the people at the pool if I was cured or not. And the man who cured me is called Jesus of Nazareth. I just talked to him in the Temple."

"Hmm. We might have known. Jesus of Nazareth, you say?"

"Yes. He . . . "

"Thank you. We'll have a talk with your Jesus. In the Temple, you say?"

"Yes."

The men went into the Temple and in a while they found Jesus.

"Sir," they said in an angry tone, "what right do you have to tell people to break the

Sabbath?"

"My Father goes on working," Jesus answered. "So do I."

"You call God your Father?"

"Yes. The Father sent me. I do nothing by myself. I do what my Father wishes."

And Jesus left them. From that time on some people were against Jesus because he broke the Sabbath—and made himself equal to God.

The Official's Daughter

THERE was a large crowd waiting for Jesus on the shore of the lake. Jesus had been preaching on the other side of the lake, in the country of the Gadarenes. He had met a man there who had many devils in him. Jesus cured the man by sending the devils into a herd of pigs. The pigs ran off the top of a hill and fell into the lake and drowned.

Word of what Jesus had done spread to all parts of the country. That is why many people were waiting for him— they wanted Jesus to cure them also.

As Jesus got out of the boat, one of the officials of the synagogue came to him and fell at his feet. His name was Jairus.

"Sir," Jairus said, almost weeping, "my little daughter is dying. Please come with me and put your hands on her. I'm sure that will make her feel better. Please save my little girl's life!"

"I will come," Jesus answered.

They began to walk toward the official's house, and the large crowd followed.

There was a woman in the crowd who had had an illness for twelve long years. The doctors had tried to help her, but they could do nothing. Now, as she saw Jesus passing near her, she thought to herself:

"If I could only touch his clothes, I'm sure I would be cured."

She pushed through the crowd. It was very difficult because the crowd was tightly surrounding Jesus. But finally she reached Jesus and touched his robe. And she was cured at once!

Jesus felt that his power had been used to cure someone, and he said, "Who touched me?"

His disciples looked at him, surprised. Why, everyone was touching Jesus! They said:

"But, Master, the crowd is pushing against you. Of course, someone touched you. They are all touching. Why do you ask?"

But Jesus kept looking around. "Someone touched me," he said.

Then the woman came closer to Jesus. She was so frightened her hands were shaking. She fell at his feet.

"Master—I . . . I touched you. But I have been suffering for such a long time. And now I am cured!"

Jesus looked down at her.

"My daughter," he said kindly, "your faith has cured you. Go, now, and don't worry. Your illness will not return."

As Jesus was speaking, some people from Jairus's house arrived.

"Jairus," they said, "we have bad news."

"My daughter!" Jairus exclaimed.

"Yes. She . . . she is dead."

Tears began to flow down Jairus's cheeks. "But . . . but Jesus is . . ."

"Don't put Jesus to any more trouble, Jairus. It is too late. Your daughter is dead."

Jesus heard what they were saying. He turned to Jairus.

"Do not be afraid," he said to the weeping man. "Have faith in me. Everything will be all right."

Then Jesus spoke to the crowd:

"You must wait here for me. I want only Peter, James, and John to go with me."

Jesus and the three disciples set out with Jairus. When they reached Jairus's house, they heard people screaming and wailing.

"Why are you making all this noise?" Jesus asked. "The girl is not dead—she is only sleeping."

The people stopped crying immediately. But then they began laughing!

"How foolish can you be?" they jeered. "The girl is dead!"

Jesus looked at them sternly. "Leave!" he said. "Out! All of you!"

And the people hurried out.

"Now, Jairus, come with me. Bring your wife, too. And, Peter, James and John—you come, too."

They went into the room where the body of the girl lay. Jesus went up to her and took her hand.

"Little girl," he said gently, "get up."

And, immediately, the girl got up and began to walk around. Then she ran to her mother.

"Do not tell anyone what

happened," Jesus said. "Now—give the child something to eat. I'm sure she is hungry."

What a marvelous thing! How happy Jairus and his wife were. The whole world should have been thankful to Jesus.

But then something strange happened. Jesus left Jairus's house and went back with his disciples to Nazareth, his home town. You would think the people of Nazareth would be the happiest people in the world. You would think that they would praise Jesus for all the wonderful things he had done.

But when Jesus spoke in the synagogue, the people began to say to each other:

"Where does this man get all these things he's saying?"

"What does he know?"

"Right! He's nothing but a carpenter. We know his parents—Mary and Joseph. They're very simple people!"

"Yes—who is Jesus trying to make himself out to be? A little praise certainly went to his head!"

Jesus was saddened. "A prophet is not accepted in his own town. How sad!"

And Jesus, who had cured Jairus's daughter, who had done so many good things, could not work any miracles in Nazareth—his own home town.

The people of Nazareth had no faith in him.

The Vision on the Mountain

ONE day Jesus took Peter, James, and John aside.

"We must go up that mountain over there," he said.

"Why, Master?" Peter asked.

"I wish to pray."

"But . . ."

"Come!" Jesus insisted. They walked to the foot of the mountain and looked up at the long climb above them.

"This will not be easy," Peter said. He was a fisherman and more accustomed to the level water.

"Come!" Jesus repeated, and he began the climb up the mountainside.

They struggled up a winding dirt path, stumbling over rocks and climbing over trees that had fallen in the path. The disciples were strong men, but they were soon a good distance behind Jesus.

"I'm worried," Peter said to James and John, gasping for breath.

"Why?" James asked.

"It is the Master. I believe in him with all my heart. I know he is the Messiah. But lately he keeps saying that he must die."

"Don't worry, Peter," James answered. "Jesus knows what he is doing."

"But—you don't think he is going to die now? On top of this mountain?"

"He said he wanted to pray, that's all," John said.

They struggled up further. They could just barely see Jesus up above them.

"Something puzzles me, though," Peter said.

"What's that?"

"They say that Elijah will return before the Messiah comes—to prepare the way. I have not seen Elijah."

"Some say John the Baptist was Elijah," James said.

"Yes. We must ask Jesus about that."

After more than an hour's climb they finally reached an open space at the top of the mountain. Jesus was at the other side of the open space, praying already. The disciples sat down and, worn out by the climb, fell asleep.

When they awoke a short time later, they saw a marvelous sight. Jesus seemed changed. His face was as bright as the sun, and his clothes as white as lightning. And then, suddenly, two men appeared, one on either side of Jesus. They were Moses and Elijah! Jesus talked with them, but the disciples could not hear what they were saying.

Peter did not know what to say, but then he blurted out, "Lord, if you want me to, I'll make three tents, one for you, and one each for Moses and Elijah."

But Jesus did not answer.

Then a thick cloud covered the top of the mountain. Everything grew dark. The disciples shook with fear.

A voice spoke from the cloud:

"Jesus is My beloved son, My chosen one. Listen to what he says."

When the disciples heard the voice they fell to the ground and hid their faces. They were completely terrified.

Then the cloud disappeared and Jesus came over to them.

"Do not be afraid," he said. "Stand up." And when the disciples looked up, they saw only Jesus.

"Do not tell anyone what you have seen until I have risen from the dead," Jesus said.

Again, the disciples were mystified. They were not sure what Jesus was saying. Then Peter asked:

"Master, isn't Elijah supposed to come before the Messiah?"

"Yes," Jesus answered. "He has come. You have seen him. But people paid no attention to him."

Then the disciples understood: Jesus was talking about John the Baptist.

The Loaves and the Fishes

JESUS and the disciples had been working very hard spreading the word of God.

"I think you should have a rest," Jesus said to the disciples. "Let us go to a quiet spot on the other side of the lake."

So they set out in the boat. But many people saw them leave and began running along the shore. As a result, by the time Jesus and the disciples arrived at the other side of the lake, a large crowd had already gathered there.

"Why don't the people understand?" Peter said. "We need some rest."

"Yes, we do," Jesus said. "But they are like sheep without anyone to lead them. Bring the boat to the shore. I will talk to them."

And Jesus spoke to the great crowd for a long time. When he finished it was almost evening.

Peter said, "Master, let the people go. This is a lonely place. They have just enough time to go to the village to buy food."

"Feed them yourselves," Jesus answered.

"What?"

"Philip!" Jesus called to another disciple. "Where can we buy some food for these people?"

"Master, do you realize how much money it would take to feed all these people—even if we only got a mouthful for each? Why, there are over five thousand people here! We can't do it!"

Then Andrew, Peter's brother, spoke up. "Master, there's a small boy here."

The boy moved to Andrew's side. He was holding a basket.

"He has five loaves of barley bread and two fishes. That is all the food we can find—not enough to feed more than a few people."

"Tell the people to sit down," Jesus said. It was a beautiful place, with plenty of grass. The people made themselves comfortable on the grass.

"Son," Jesus said to the boy, "bring your basket here." The boy shyly approached Jesus and gave him the basket. "Fine. Thank you. Now you can sit down, too."

Then Jesus took the loaves and prayed over them. He did the same with the fishes.

"Give these out to the people," he said to the disciples.

The disciples passed through the crowd, handing out pieces of bread and fish.

"Not too much, there!" a disciple said to one man. "We have a lot of people to feed!"

"Let them take as much as they want," Jesus called. "There will be plenty."

The disciples couldn't believe what was happening. No matter how much of the bread or the fish they gave to one person, there was always enough for the next!

The people began to look at each other. "Whatever is happening?" they said.

When the disciples finished, they came back to Jesus and sat down and began to eat also. But it was difficult to eat—they were too astounded by what had just happened. The bread and fish had multiplied in their very own hands!

Then Jesus said, "Now, go and collect the crumbs, so that nothing will be wasted."

The disciples did as they were told, and before they had finished they had collected more than twelve large baskets of crumbs!

Then all the people began to shout, "No one is like Jesus! We must make him king!"

But Jesus slipped away quickly and hid himself in the hills. He knew his time had not come yet!

The Good Samaritan

ONE day a lawyer came to Jesus. The man was proud of his learning and he wanted to see if he could confuse Jesus.

"Master," he said, "what must I do if I want to go to heaven after I die?"

"You are an intelligent man," Jesus said. "You read the scriptures. What does the law of God say?"

"It says: 'You must love the Lord your God with all your heart and with all your soul, with all your strength and with all your mind. And you must love your neighbor as you love yourself.' "

"That is a correct answer," Jesus said. "Do that, and you will have eternal life."

But the man was not satisfied. Jesus had answered that question too easily. He tried another question:

"But, Master, who is my neighbor?"

Then Jesus told this story:

Once there was a man who was traveling on the road from Jerusalem to Jericho. About halfway to Jericho, a group of bandits ran out from behind some bushes.

"Give us everything you have!" they threatened.

The man gave them all his money. But the bandits were not satisfied. They beat up the man and left him, half dead, on the road.

A little while later, a priest came along. He saw the man lying on the road, but he did not want to be bothered. So he walked around the man and continued on his way.

Still later, a Levite came by. He saw the man, too, but said to himself, "Something dangerous has happened here. I'd better get out of here fast!" And he hurried by the man.

Finally, another man came down the road, riding a donkey. He was a Samaritan. He saw the man lying in the road. But he did not pass by. He jumped down from his donkey.

"What happened to you?" he asked. But the wounded man was too weak to answer.

The Samaritan cleaned the man's wounds and covered them with bandages. Then, gently, he lifted the man onto the donkey and brought him to the nearest inn.

That night he sat up with the man, helping him as much as possible. Slowly, the man began to recover.

But the next morning the Samaritan had to continue his journey. The man was better, but still not well enough to walk. So the Samaritan gave the innkeeper twenty dollars and said:

"Look, do everything that is necessary for that poor man, until he is well enough to go home. On my way back, I'll pay you anything you have spent over twenty dollars." The innkeeper agreed and the Samaritan rode off.

When Jesus had finished the story, he turned to the lawyer.

"Which of the three men," he asked, "was a true neighbor to the man who was attacked by the bandits?"

"Well—," the lawyer answered, "you know we Jews do not like the Samaritans. They are low people. But I guess I would have to say that the Samaritan was the true neighbor."

"You have answered well," Jesus said. "Now you would do well to imitate that good Samaritan."

The Unforgiving Servant

JESUS often taught that people should forgive each other. But Peter had a doubt about this, and one day he asked Jesus:

"Master, I know you have taught that I must forgive everyone. But how many *times* should I forgive? Would seven times be enough?"

"No," Jesus said, "not seven times, but seventy times seven. There should be no special number of times. You should forgive *always*."

Then Jesus told this story:

Once upon a time there was a king who was very wealthy and very powerful. He often used to lend money to his servants when they needed it. But, one day, he was looking through his book of accounts and he noticed that some servants had borrowed large amounts of money and had never paid anything back.

"Hmmm," he thought to himself, "I'll have to do something about this."

He called his chief servant. "Here," he commanded, "take this book and send me all the people who owe me money. I want to clear all this up tomorrow."

The chief servant did as he was told, and the next morning he brought a man into the king.

"Here, sir," he said to the king, "is a servant who owes you nine million dollars."

"That is a huge sum of money," the king said to the servant. "I want you to pay me back at once!"

"But, my lord . . ."

"You are not willing to pay the debt?"

"Yes, sir, I am. But . . ."

"But what?"

"I don't have any money right now. I can't pay."

"What did you do with all that

money I lent you?"

"I . . . I . . ." The man could not answer.

"Well—we'll see about this! Chief servant, come here! Take this man! You are to sell him and his wife and his children and all his possessions. At least I'll get *some* of my money back!"

But the man threw himself down at the king's feet. "Please," he pleaded. "Please—just give me a little time. I will pay you everything I owe. Please don't sell my wife and my children. Have pity on us."

And the king felt sorry for the man. "Oh, the money doesn't mean that much to me," he said. "You can go. I forgive you the

debt."

"Sir?" The servant couldn't believe his ears.

"You heard me. You owe me nothing!"

"Oh, my lord, how can I . . . Sir, I'll never forget this. I . . ."

"Now get out of here before I change my mind!" the king commanded.

"Yes. Yes, sir. Right away." And the servant ran from the room.

Now, as the servant was leaving the king's palace, he met another servant.

"Hey!" he shouted after him. "You owe me fifteen dollars. When are you going to pay me?"

"I . . . I . . ."

201

The servant grabbed his fellow servant by the throat and almost choked him. "Pay me my fifteen dollars!"

But the man fell to his knees. "I don't have it now. Give me time and I'll pay you."

"No—not on your life!"

"But I can get it! It's just that my son is sick now and . . ."

"No excuses! You owe me fifteen dollars and I want it! Now!"

"Well, I can't *pay* now."

"Then off to prison with you!"

"Prison?"

"Yes! And you can rot there until I get my fifteen dollars!"

And the man was put in prison.

Very soon the other servants heard what had happened. "Something ought to be done about this," they said.

"Yes! Did you ever hear anything so terrible? The king forgives this man a nine-million dollar debt and he turns around and throws a fellow servant in jail for fifteen dollars. Fifteen dollars!"

"Well, I think someone should tell the king."

The servants decided to tell the king. The king was furious when he heard the story.

"I can't believe it!" he said. "Send that man to me!"

The man was brought in.

"You are a wicked man," the king said. "I forgave you every penny of your debt because I felt pity for you and your family. Couldn't you have any pity for your own fellow servant?"

But the man could not answer.

"Send him to the dungeons," the king roared. "Let the torturers take care of him! And you—you wicked man—you'll not get out until I have every penny you owe me!"

When Jesus finished the story, he said, "That is how God will treat you unless you forgive each other in your heart."

The Man Born Blind

JESUS and his disciples were walking near the Temple in Jerusalem. They saw a man sitting at the side of the path, begging. He was blind.

"I've seen that man here before," one of the disciples said. "They say he was born blind."

"Master," another disciple asked, "who sinned? Was it this man or his parents? Whose sin was it that made him be born blind?"

"He did not sin," Jesus said, "nor did his parents. He was born blind so that everyone might now see God's power."

"God's power?"

"Yes. I am the light of the world. I must do the work that the Father has sent me to do."

And Jesus bent over and spat on the ground. Then he made a paste of the spittle and dirt and rubbed the paste on the man's eyes.

"What is happening?" the blind man asked.

"Go to the pool of Siloam," Jesus said to the blind man. "Wash your eyes with the water of the pool."

The man walked to the pool. He walked slowly so as not to stumble and fall. When he arrived at the pool, he had someone help him to the water. There he splashed his eyes and then looked up. Slowly, the world took on shapes—trees, buildings, people . . .

"I can see!" he screamed. "I can see!" And he ran off toward his house, still shouting, "I can see!"

The people that he passed said to each other, "Isn't that the man who used to sit and beg?"

"Yes, it is!" one said.

"No! No, it can't be. It only looks like him," another disagreed.

"But I'm sure it's he!"

The man heard them and shouted, "Yes! It's me! I'm the one! But now I can see! Oh, the world is beautiful!"

"How come you can see now?" they asked him.

"A man named Jesus put some paste on my eyes. 'Go the pool of Siloam,' he said. And I went and I washed my eyes. And now I can see! I can see!"

"Where is this Jesus?"

"Why—I don't know!"

"This is very extraordinary. Come, we should go to the religious leaders and tell them about this."

And they brought the man who had been blind to some of the religious leaders.

"Sirs, we would like you to hear this man's story."

"What happened?" one of the leaders said.

The man who had been blind proudly repeated his story: "Jesus made a paste and covered my eyes and told me to wash in the pool of Siloam. And now I can see!"

"Hmm. Then this man cannot be from God," one of the leaders said.

"Not from God! But why?"

"He made the paste on the Sabbath. It is against the law to do any work, no matter how small, on the Sabbath. Any man who breaks the law cannot be a man of God!"

"But," another leader said, "how could a sinner do such a wonderful thing? I think you are wrong. Jesus must be from God."

"No! The letter of the law must be obeyed. If a man breaks the law, he is a sinner. Jesus broke the law. He is a sinner!"

"But I don't agree. There must be some exception . . ."

"There are no exceptions to the law!"

"But this man was born blind—and now he sees!"

"I don't care!"

Then one of the leaders turned back to the blind man. "What do you have to say?" he asked. "You were cured. What do you think about this Jesus?"

"I think he is a prophet."

"Ha! What do you know?"

"Wait!" One of the leaders held up his hand. "How do we know this man is telling the truth? There are plenty of beggars, mind you, who fake blindness so people will give them money."

"But I was born blind!"

"Your word is not proof enough. We will talk to your parents."

The man's parents were sent

for, and when they arrived they were asked by the leaders:

"Is this man your son?"

"Yes, sirs," the parents answered very nervously.

"Was he born blind?"

"Yes."

"Then how is it that he can see now?"

The parents held up their hands. "We know he is our son and that he was born blind. How he can see now, or who opened his eyes—we don't know. Why don't you ask him? Surely, he's old enough to answer for himself."

The leaders turned to the man again. "Man, give praise to God," they said. "We know this Jesus is a sinner."

"I don't know if he's a sinner or not," the man answered. "All I know is that I was blind and now I can see!"

"What did he do? How did he cure you?"

"I already told you," the man said, "and you wouldn't listen to me. Why do you want to hear it all again? Do you want to be his followers, too?"

"How dare you talk like that!" the leaders said. "You can be his follower. We are followers of Moses! God spoke to Moses—we know that. But this man Jesus—

we don't know where he comes from."

"Well, I'm surprised at you!" The man grew in courage every time he spoke. "This man cures

my blindness and you don't know where he comes from?"

"No, we don't!"

"But we know that God doesn't listen to sinners. He only listens to those who obey Him. And look—look in all your books! Never—since the beginning of the world—has a man born blind ever been cured! If Jesus weren't from God, then he could never have done such a thing! I can SEE! Jesus is from God!"

"Are you trying to teach us?" the leaders said angrily. "You— you're nothing but a sinner. You've never been anything but a sinner since the day you were born!"

The man who had been born blind shrugged his shoulders and left the leaders.

A short time later he passed Jesus in the street. He did not recognize Jesus because he had been blind and had never seen him. But Jesus stopped him and said:

"Do you believe in the Son of God?"

"Sir, tell me who he is so I can believe."

"You are looking at him," Jesus said. "I am the Son of God."

"Lord," the man said, "I believe!"

The Prodigal Son

ORE and more, some of the religious leaders complained that Jesus made friends with sinners and ate with them. So one day Jesus told them this story:

Once there was a man who had two sons. He was quite a rich man. He had a large ranch and a large house. Both of his sons helped him with the work, but the older son was a steadier worker. The younger son was always dreaming about far-away places.

Everyone in the family was quite happy, but the younger son could not stop dreaming about a better life he might find far away.

"Just think," he told his older brother one day. "The world is so big. There must be places better than this, places with greener grass and bluer skies."

"You dream too much," the older brother said. "I wish you'd work as hard as you dream."

"You'll see—someday I'll go. I'll live like a king!"

"We live very well here, I think. But if you're going to go, I wish you'd do it and get it over with. You're not helping me with all your talk!"

"You know, I think I'll just do that! I'm going to see father."

And the younger brother went to his father and said:

"Father, I know someday you will give me half of your riches."

"That is right, my son. You will get half and your brother will get half. Why do you mention that now?"

"Father—er—I would like my half now."

"Now!"

"Yes. I want to travel. I want to go places, see things. I want to feel free and alive."

"You are such a dreamer!"

"But, father, I am serious!"

The father looked at his son for a long while. Finally, he said:

"If that is the way it must be . . . all right. You can have your share. You can go."

"Oh, thank you, father!"

And the younger son packed his things. The next day, he left for a country far, far away.

In that country the son lived like a king indeed! He did no work, but only things that gave him pleasure. Little by little all his money disappeared.

Within a year the son suffered two disasters. That distant country, the country of his dreams, had a famine and it was hard to find food. And then, all his money was gone! He had spent every cent.

And now his stomach began to hurt him from hunger. It got so bad that he had to look for work. He took a job feeding pigs for a farmer! And he thought to himself:

"The pigs eat better than I do! I'd gladly eat their food!"

But no one would give him food, and he made too little money to buy very much.

After he had suffered like this for a while, he thought to himself: "I am dying of hunger! And my father's servants—the very servants!—have more than they can eat. I'm going back home! I'll tell father that I have sinned against him and against God. That's what I'll do! I'll ask my father to let me be one of his servants."

And he began the long journey back home.

He was still a long way down the road when his father saw him. And the father ran as fast as he could to his son! He hugged him and kissed him!

"Father," the son said, "I have sinned against you and against God. I don't deserve to be called your son."

But his father wouldn't listen. Instead, he called to his servants:

"Hurry! Bring me the best clothes and a ring and sandals! And kill a calf. We're going to have a feast! My son is back! He was dead and now he is alive again! He was lost and now he is found!"

And the servants hurried off to prepare the celebration!

The older brother was out in the fields. As he came closer to the house he heard music and saw the servants bustling back and forth.

"What's happening?" he asked one of the servants.

"Why—your brother is back!

We are going to have a feast!"

"What! How can this be! He has wasted everything—and now we are going to have a feast? Not me! I will not go near the house!"

The servants told the father about how angry the older brother was. The father came out of the house and walked toward him.

"Son, you must celebrate, too!"

"I will not! All these years I've worked hard for you. I never ran away. Where is my feast? This other son of yours—he spends all his money and comes back—he does no work—and you—agh! you make a feast for *him*!"

"But, my son, you are always with me. Everything I have is yours. But now we must celebrate! You must be happy, too! Your brother was dead and is alive again! He was lost—and now we have found him!"

When he finished the story, Jesus said to the religious leaders, "Now you know how merciful my Heavenly Father is."

How to Pray

JESUS prayed every day during his life. No matter how busy he was, he always found time to talk with his Father in heaven.

One day, when Jesus was finishing a prayer, one of his disciples said to him, "Master, teach us how to pray."

Jesus answered, "Pray with these words:

Our Father
which art in heaven,
Hallowed be thy name.
Thy kingdom come.
Thy will be done,
  as in heaven,
  so on earth.
Give us day by day
  our daily bread.
And forgive us our sins;
  for we also forgive
  everyone
That is indebted to us.
And lead us not
  into temptation;
but deliver us from evil."

Then Jesus told the disciples a story to show them how to pray:

Once there was a man who was visited by an old friend. The old friend came late at night when the man had finished supper and done the dishes. In fact, the man had nothing left to eat in the house. He was very embarrassed. So he said to his friend:

"Excuse me. I'll be right back. I have to see a neighbor."

And the man went down the street to a neighbor's house. He could see that the door was locked, but there was still a small light in the room upstairs.

"Hello!" the man called. "I need some bread!"

A muffled voice answered from upstairs: "It's too late!"

"But I need it!"

A man stuck his head out the window. "It's too late!" he said. His head disappeared back into

213

the room.

"But a friend has just arrived from a journey and I have nothing to offer him!"

The man's head popped out again.

"Look! The door's locked and my children are in bed. I can't help you." The head disappeared again.

"But you've got to help me! Whom else can I ask?"

The voice came from inside the room: "Are you going to stay there all night?"

"Please!"

There was pause. Then the lock on the door clicked and the door opened.

"Here!" the man said. "Here are three loaves. Now—please—leave me in peace."

"Thank you. You're so kind!"

Jesus smiled. "You must pray just the way the man asked for bread. Never give up! And God will always answer."

Zacchaeus

YOU'RE a mean man, Zacchaeus!"

"Business is business, my dear man," Zacchaeus answered. He was sitting behind the old desk in his office. The man standing before him was red with rage.

"All you tax collectors are wretched people. But you—you, Zacchaeus—you're worst of them all!"

"Calm down, now. You know I must do my job."

"Your job! You collect money for those Romans! Bah! Your job! You do much more than you have to. You're a thief! You cheat the poor!"

Zacchaeus sighed. "My dear man, are you going to pay your debt?"

"You know I can't pay. Both my wife and my children are sick. I hardly have enough to buy food for them."

People began gathering in the street. They could hear the man shouting.

"Ah, yes." Zacchaeus sighed again. "You told me that before. I'm very sorry, but, you see, I must . . ."

"Very sorry! Hah! That's a laugh. You don't care whether my family lives or dies! You're rich. You stole your money from the poor! And now you live in that grand house of yours!"

"Right!" some of the people outside the door shouted.

"You tell him!"

"His heart's as small as he is!"

This remark stung Zacchaeus. He was very, very small. He stood up now in anger, and everyone began pointing at him and laughing.

"Get out of here!" Zacchaeus screeched. "Get away!"

But they did not move, and the laughter would have continued if someone at the back of the crowd had not shouted:

"Here comes Jesus of Nazareth!"

Everyone ran down the street toward Jesus.

Zacchaeus thought to himself, "I want to see this wonder-worker too." And on his short, bandy legs he ran after the crowd.

But when he reached the crowd it had already completely surrounded Jesus. Zacchaeus ran around the crowd, jumping here, trying to elbow his way through there. But no one would budge an inch—especially not for Zacchaeus!

Then Zacchaeus spotted a sycamore tree. "I know what I'll do," he said to himself. And he ran and climbed the tree.

When Jesus came closer to the tree, he looked up.

"Zacchaeus," he called, "what are you doing up there?"

The crowd laughed. "He's too short to see you from the ground!"

"Zacchaeus," Jesus called again, "come down! Hurry! I want to stay in your house today."

The crowd stared and gasped. "Zacchaeus's house!"

"He's the meanest man in town!"

"How can you stay at *his* house?"

Zacchaeus fairly tumbled out of the tree. No one had ever asked to come to his house! He pushed his way to Jesus. Then he looked into Jesus' eyes and he felt his whole being change. With tears in his eyes he said:

"Lord—I . . . I don't know . . . what to . . . Lord, I will give half of everything I own to the poor. And—and if I have cheated anyone, I will pay him back— four times the amount I owe!"

Jesus smiled and spoke to the crowd. "Zacchaeus is a son of God, too. I came to save everyone. Zacchaeus was lost— that is why I came to him."

Let the Children Come to Me

EVERYONE in Israel, it seemed, had now heard of Jesus. They heard of the wonderful things he did and the wise things he said.

People came from all over to see him. And many people brought their children to Jesus.

"Get as close to him as you can," parents would tell their children. "I want Jesus to touch you."

And the parents would push their children through the crowds. The children, of course, obeyed their parents. But the children sometimes became a bother. They would push right up to Jesus, sometimes they leaned on his knee, and at times they interrupted Jesus when he was talking.

The disciples were disturbed because of the trouble the children caused.

"Get back, children! Let Jesus talk. You parents—can't you control your children?"

But when Jesus heard the disciples talking in this way, he said:

"Let the children come to me. Don't stop them. The kingdom of God belongs to them. You older people—you must become like children, innocent and joyful, to enter God's kingdom."

The Raising of Lazarus

JESUS had many friends, but Lazarus and his two sisters, Mary and Martha, were special friends. They lived about two miles from Jerusalem in a town called Bethany.

One day Lazarus became very sick. Martha and Mary were very worried because nothing seemed to help him. Each day he became worse, and his sisters were afraid that he might die. They asked a friend:

"Would you go to Jesus and tell him that Lazarus is very, very sick?"

The friend went gladly. He found Jesus on the other side of the Jordan River. When he gave Jesus the message, Jesus said:

"This sickness will not end in death. The sickness will give glory to God and the Son of God."

But Jesus did not say anything more. And, even though he loved Lazarus, he did not go to Bethany right away. In fact, he did not even mention Lazarus's sickness for two whole days. Then, finally, he said to his disciples:

"Now we will go to Bethany."

This worried the disciples. "Master," one said, "you know how close Bethany is to Jerusalem."

"You know," another continued, "that some people in those parts want to kill you."

"It's too dangerous to go there now."

Jesus answered, "I have only a short time to do what I must do. Lazarus, our friend, is resting. I must go to wake him up."

These words confused the disciples. "If Lazarus is resting," they said, "he must be getting better. The rest will do him a world of good."

"You did not understand me," Jesus answered. "Lazarus is

dead."

"Dead?"

"Yes. And for your sake I'm glad I wasn't there. What I will do now will help you believe. Come, we must go."

Then one of the disciples, named Thomas, said to the others, "I know it's dangerous. But if Jesus is going to be killed—let us go and die with him!"

All agreed, and they began walking toward Bethany. By the time they arrived near the town, Lazarus had already been in the tomb four days.

Since Jerusalem is so close to Bethany, many people had come to console Martha and Mary.

"He was a good man, Martha," one would say.

"Yes, I know."

"He will be missed."

Then a friend came to Martha and said, "Jesus is coming!"

Martha got up immediately and ran down the road to meet Jesus.

"Martha!" Jesus called to her when he saw her coming.

"Master! Oh, Master! If only you had been here, Lazarus wouldn't have died," Martha sobbed.

"Lazarus will rise again."

"Yes, Master, I know he will rise again on the last day."

"I am the resurrection," Jesus said. "If a person believes in me, then even though he dies, he will live. If anyone believes in me, he will never die. Do you believe that?"

"Yes, Master, I believe. You are the Son of God. I believe . . . Oh, Master—I forgot. Excuse me. I must go and call Mary."

Martha ran back to the house. "Mary, Mary," she whispered to her sister, "Jesus is here."

Mary got up at once and went out with Martha. The people who were there did not hear what Martha had said.

"They must be going to the tomb," they said. "Come! Let us go with them."

Mary ran directly to Jesus and fell at his feet, sobbing.

"Oh, Jesus," she said. "If only you had been here, Lazarus would still be alive!"

Now tears welled up in Jesus' eyes. "Where have you buried him?"

"Come and see," Mary answered.

Then tears streamed down Jesus' face.

The people who had followed Martha and Mary from the house remarked, "Look! Jesus is

221

weeping!"

"He must have loved Lazarus very much."

But others said, "He cured a man born blind in Jerusalem. If he loved Lazarus so much, why didn't he come sooner and cure him?"

Jesus went with Martha and Mary to the tomb. The people followed.

Lazarus was buried in a cave, as most Jews were in those days. A large stone had been rolled up to the mouth of the cave, to seal it.

"Roll the stone away," Jesus said.

"But, Lord!" Martha said. "The body has been in the tomb four days! It will . . ."

"I told you," Jesus interrupted, "that if you believe you will see God's glory."

"Yes, Lord."

"Roll the stone away."

The stone was large and heavy but, finally, some of the men were able to move it away from the mouth of the cave. Then they stepped back.

Jesus raised his eyes toward heaven. "Father," he said, "thank You for hearing my prayer. I know You always hear me, but I want everyone standing here to listen to this prayer so that they may believe it is You who sent me."

Then Jesus called out in a loud voice:

"Lazarus! Come out!"

The crowd gasped as Lazarus appeared at the mouth of the cave. Lazarus was wrapped in the narrow white cloths that were used in those days to clothe the bodies of the dead.

"Take the cloths off," Jesus said. "Let him go free."

And with great shouts of joy the men freed Lazarus and took him back to the house.

Many of the people who were there that day and saw what Jesus had done believed in him. But others, when they had returned to Jerusalem, went to the religious leaders and told them what Jesus had done.

The religious leaders held a meeting.

"This Jesus is doing all these things, and what are we doing about it?" one said.

"Mark my words, if we let him continue, everyone will believe in him!"

"Yes! And the Romans won't like that."

"Not one bit! They'll be worried that Jesus is trying to take over the government. In no time they'll be here with troops. They'll destroy us all!"

"Right!"

One of the leaders, Caiaphas, who was high priest that year, said, "I don't think you really understand the problem. There is only one solution. It is better for one man to die for the people than for all the people to be slaughtered."

The leaders agreed. And from that moment they were determined to kill Jesus.

Jesus Enters Jerusalem

JESUS went with his disciples toward Jerusalem. When they were still a short distance from the city, near a village called Bethphage, Jesus said:

"Go into this village. You will find a colt tied up there. The colt has never been ridden yet. Bring it here."

"And if someone asks why we are taking the colt?"

"Tell them the Master needs it."

The disciples went into the village. And there, in the center of town, was a colt tied to a pole.

"Has this colt ever been ridden?" the disciples asked some men standing nearby.

"Never."

"Good!" And they began to untie the colt.

"Hey!" one of the men yelled at them. "What are you doing, untying that colt?"

"The Master needs it."

The man nodded and said nothing more.

The disciples took the colt to Jesus. Then they took off their cloaks and threw them over the back of the colt. They helped Jesus up on the animal.

Word had spread throughout Jerusalem that Jesus was coming. Many had heard how he had returned Lazarus to life and they wanted to see Jesus. They crowded the road leading into Jerusalem.

And as Jesus rode into the city, the people put their cloaks on the road in front of him. They also cut down branches from the trees and covered the road with them. And they began to shout:

"Hosanna! Blessed be
the king who comes
in the name of the Lord!"

Some of the religious leaders were disturbed by this. They went up to Jesus.

"Sir! Please tell these followers of yours to quiet down. The Romans will not like this."

"If the people keep quiet," Jesus answered them, "then the stones will cheer."

The leaders went off, talking angrily to one another.

"See, there is nothing we can do!"

"The whole world is running after this Jesus!"

"We must do something to get rid of him!"

The Last Supper

IT WAS the time of the great feast of the Passover. The Jews eat a special meal on this feast day. It recalls the time when God saved them from the Egyptians and brought them into the promised land.

The disciples said to Jesus, "Where do you want us to prepare for the Passover meal?"

"Go into Jerusalem," Jesus said, "and you will see a man carrying a pitcher of water. Follow him and watch what house he goes into. Then say to the owner of that house: 'The Master wants to know where the room is that he can use for the Passover meal.' He will show you. Prepare the meal there."

The disciples did as they were told, and that evening Jesus and his disciples gathered in the room for the meal.

Jesus stood up and took off his outer cloak. Then he wrapped a towel around his waist and prepared to wash his disciples' feet.

When Peter saw this, he said, "Master, are you going to wash *my* feet?"

"I know, Peter," Jesus answered, "you do not understand now, but you will later."

"No, Master, never! You won't wash my feet!"

Jesus looked up at Peter. "If I don't wash your feet, then you can have nothing more to do with me."

"Oh! Then—then wash all of me!"

"No, Peter, it will be enough to wash your feet."

When he had finished, Jesus sat down and they all began to eat. While they were eating, Jesus said:

"One of you will betray me."

This shocked the disciples. They looked at each other. It wasn't possible! Peter turned to

John, who was sitting next to Jesus.

"Ask him who it is," he whispered.

John asked Jesus and Jesus said, "It is the one to whom I give this piece of bread." Then he leaned over and gave the bread to Judas. "Go and do what you have planned. Do it quickly."

The other disciples did not understand what was happening. When Judas left, they thought he had gone to buy some food that had been forgotten. But Judas knew. He had bargained with the chief religious leaders.

They had promised him thirty pieces of silver if he betrayed Jesus.

When Judas had left, Jesus took some bread, said a blessing over it, and then broke it. He gave it to the disciples and said:

"This is my body. Take it."

Then he took some wine, blessed it, and gave it to them.

"This is my blood. It will be shed for many, many people."

Then they said the prayers that are customary in the Passover meal. The meal was finished.

Then Jesus said sadly, "You will all lose faith in me. You will run away. But do not worry. After I rise from the dead, I will see you again in Galilee."

Peter was deeply hurt that Jesus had said this. "No, Master! That is not true! Even if everyone else deserts you, I will not!"

Jesus turned to Peter. "Mark my words, Peter," he said. "Tonight—yes, this very night— you will deny me three times. Before the rooster crows twice, you will deny me three times!"

"Never! Even if I die with you, I will never deny you!" Peter answered.

Jesus look sadly at Peter. "Come," he said. "We must go."

The Garden of Olives

JESUS and the disciples left the upper room where they had eaten the Passover meal and began walking toward a place called Gethsemane.

They had to walk down a dirt path that had steps dug into it, then across the Kidron Brook. The brook rarely had much water in it, so Jesus and the disciples were able to cross it easily. On the other side of the brook they came to a small garden that was surrounded by stones and olive trees. It was a quiet place, and since it was late at night no one would bother them here.

Jesus turned to his disciples and said, "Wait here. I want to go into the garden to pray."

But then he turned to Peter, James, and John, and said, "You may come with me."

The four of them walked into the garden. When they were out of sight of the others, Jesus said to Peter, James, and John:

"Wait here. Keep awake."

"Yes, Master."

"I feel very, very sad."

Then Jesus moved alone farther into the garden. He fell down with his face to the ground and began to pray.

"Father," he said, "if it is possible, spare me this suffering. But—let Your will be done."

He remained praying for a while, then got up and came back to Peter, James, and John. But, because it was so late, they had not been able to keep their eyes open.

"Can't you stay awake one hour with me?"

The disciples struggled to their feet, trying not to yawn.

"You should stay awake and pray. Pray that you be not tempted."

They wiped the sleep from their eyes and tried to stand

erect.

Jesus left them again and returned to the spot where he had prayed before.

"My Father," he said, "if it is not possible that I be spared this suffering, then—Your will be done!"

He returned to the disciples a second time. Again, they were fast asleep. Jesus looked down at them but decided not to wake them this time. He left them there and returned to his prayer. Then an angel appeared to Jesus to give him courage and comfort. But Jesus continued to pray, and he prayed with such agony that his sweat became drops of blood and fell to the ground. Jesus knew the suffering that he would soon have to endure.

After a long while, he got up again and returned to the disciples. They were sleeping even more soundly this time.

"You should have been awake and praying for strength," he said softly. "You need strength to face what you must tonight. But it is too late." Then, loudly, he said, "Get up now! Let us go!"

The disciples stirred themselves.

"Come!" Jesus said. "Judas, my betrayer, is close by!"

The Capture

JUDAS knew where to find Jesus. He had often gone to the Garden of Olives with Jesus and the other disciples. He now crossed the Kidron Brook with a group of soldiers. They all carried torches and swords.

"Remember what I told you," Judas said. "The one whom I kiss is Jesus. Seize him."

Judas thought about how all this had been arranged. A few days before he had gone to the chief priests and had said to them:

"What will you give me if I hand Jesus over to you?"

The priests consulted among themselves for a few minutes. Then one said, "We will pay you thirty pieces of silver."

"I will do it!"

And Judas made all the arrangements. He knew that the best time would be after the Passover meal. It would be dark, and he was certain Jesus would go to the Garden of Olives. There would be no people in that place to give the soldiers any trouble.

"Come now!" Judas said. "Into the garden!"

The soldiers entered the garden in a rush. Jesus came right towards them.

"Whom are you looking for?" he asked.

"Jesus of Nazareth," they answered.

"I am he."

Then the soldiers felt a strong, invisible force push them back. They fell to the ground in confusion.

Judas moved toward Jesus. "Good evening, Master," he said. Then he kissed Jesus.

"Will you betray me with a kiss, Judas?" Jesus asked.

Only then did the disciples realize what was happening. Peter pulled out his sword. He

ran at a soldier, who happened to be the high priest's personal guard. With one swipe of his sword, Peter cut the man's ear off.

"Enough of that!" Jesus commanded. "Don't you think that, if I wanted it, my Father could send an army of angels to defend me? Put your sword away! He who lives by the sword, will die by the sword."

Then Jesus went up to the injured man and touched him and cured him.

The other soldiers surrounded Jesus and held him tightly.

"Must you come with swords to capture me?" Jesus said. "Every day you could have seen me in the Temple. You never tried to touch me then. But go ahead; this is your night. Only, do not harm these others. They have done nothing."

As if these words were some kind of signal, the disciples began to run away. The soldiers tried to stop them, but the disciples were too quick. One disciple, who was wearing only a loose outer cloak, was almost caught. A soldier grabbed his cloak, but the disciple wriggled out of it and ran off—naked.

Then the soldiers forced Jesus to walk with them to the high priest's house. All the chief priests were waiting for him there.

Jesus on Trial

THE soldiers who had captured Jesus in the Garden of Olives brought him to the home of Caiaphas, the high priest. Peter followed along at a distance. He did not want to be caught, but he had to see what the religious leaders were going to do to Jesus.

All the chief priests and religious leaders were gathered in Caiaphas's house. When Jesus was brought in, they made him stand in the middle of the room. The trial began.

Several witnesses spoke against Jesus, but they were obviously lying. Then two more men spoke.

"This man said he would destroy the Temple and rebuild it in three days," they charged.

"Did you hear that?" Caiaphas said. "Jesus—do you have any answer to that?"

But Jesus remained silent.

"I see we're not getting anywhere at all," Caiphas said. "Let's get down to the heart of the matter. Jesus, I want you to tell me under oath if you are the Messiah, the Son of God."

"I am," Jesus answered.

"There you have it!" Caiaphas screamed. "He has made himself equal to God! He deserves death for that!"

"Yes! Yes! Death!" everyone shouted in agreement.

Then they blindfolded Jesus and the guards spat at him and hit him.

"Ha! Jesus!" they mocked him. "You're a great prophet. Tell us who hit you that time!"

But Jesus remained silent.

"Take him to Pilate for a Roman trial!" Caiaphas commanded.

Outside, in the courtyard, Peter was warming himself at the open fire. In the distance he could hear a rooster crowing.

A servant girl came up to

Peter and said:

"I think I recognize you. You were always with Jesus. I'm sure I've seen you."

"Don't be foolish, girl," Peter said. "I don't even know this Jesus." He felt afraid.

But then another girl said, "No, I'm positive. I saw you with Jesus many times."

"Will you stop talking like that?" Peter answered. "You have nothing in your head! I don't have anything to do with Jesus!"

"I think you're lying," a man said. "Why—you talk like a Galilean. This Jesus is from Galilee, too. You are one of Jesus' disciples."

"No!" Peter shouted. "I swear I am not a disciple of Jesus!"

Then the rooster crowed a second time.

At that moment, the door opened and the guards brought Jesus out. As Jesus passed Peter, he stopped for a moment and looked deeply into Peter's eyes. Then Peter remembered what Jesus had said: "Before the rooster crows twice, you will deny me three times."

Tears flowed down Peter's rough face.

In the meanwhile, Judas, who had betrayed Jesus, went back to the chief priests who had given him money.

"Here!" he said. "Take your money back. I am ashamed of

what I have done!"

"It's a little late for that," the chief priests said. "You keep the money."

"No!" Judas shouted, and threw the thirty pieces of silver on the floor. Then he ran out and hanged himself from a tree.

Pilate, the Roman governor, brought Jesus into a private room.

"Look," he said. "I'm tired of all these religious problems you Jews have. The men who brought you here said you call yourself the king of the Jews. Are you the king of the Jews?"

"Yes."

"Are all these other things they say against you true also?"

Jesus remained silent.

"Look—answer me! Do you know I have the power to put you to death?"

"You would have no power at all if God didn't give it to you."

"Bah! Religious riddles!"

A servant entered the room. "A message from your wife, Pilate," he said.

Pilate took the note and read it. "Don't have anything to do with this man," it said. "I have had bad dreams about him."

"What a mess," Pilate muttered. "Now she has bad dreams! Jesus, you wait here. I'm going out to talk to these people."

Pilate went out to the chief priests.

"Gentlemen," he said, "I think I have a solution to this whole problem. It's Passover time—your great feast. Now, I usually release a prisoner every Passover. This year, I'll give you a choice. You can have this man, Jesus, or you can have Barabbas."

The chief priests muttered. Barabbas? Why, was there any worse criminal in Israel? Who wanted him in the streets again? But . . .

Then they began to shout:

"Give us Barabbas!"

"And what should I do with Jesus?" Pilate asked.

"Crucify him!"

"But why? What harm has he done?"

"Crucify him! Crucify him!"

Pilate called for a bowl of water. He washed his hands in it and said, "Look—I wash my hands of this whole matter. I'm not taking any responsibility for this."

"We'll take the blame! Crucify him!"

"All right. I will have Jesus crucified!"

The Cross

PILATE handed Jesus over to the Roman soldiers.

"Come," they said, "let's have some fun with him."

They pulled Jesus' clothes off and put a scarlet cloak on him.

"Here! Make a crown for him with this," a soldier said, holding up a thorny bush.

"Great!"

They formed branches into a crown and then placed it on Jesus' head. Then they put a stick in his hand. "That's your scepter!"

They all bowed low.

"Hail, O great king of the Jews! Ha! Ha! Ha!"

And they spat at Jesus and hit him on the head with sticks.

"The scourging!"

"Yes, the scourging!"

They took the cloak off Jesus and tied him by the hands to a low post. And they whipped him without mercy.

When they had finished, they put Jesus' own clothes back on him and led him out to crucify him.

They made Jesus carry the heavy beam of wood that would be part of his cross. Jesus almost stumbled when they put it on him.

"Steady there! You've got a walk before you yet. Then you can rest. Ha! Ha! Ha!"

Jesus was very weak. Strong men had died from Roman whippings. After walking for a while, Jesus stumbled and fell.

"He's not going to make it," a soldier said, "not if he has to carry that beam."

"Well, get someone to carry it for him," another soldier said.

And they pointed to a man in the crowd that had gathered along the side of the street.

"Hey, you! Come here! What's your name?"

"Simon."

238

"All right, Simon. You carry the beam."

"But . . ."

"Carry it!"

With Simon's help, Jesus was able to reach the place called Golgotha.

There, the soldiers nailed Jesus' hands and feet to the cross and lifted the cross into place.

"Hey! Look at this robe!" one of the soldiers said. "I think I'll take it for myself!"

"Wait a minute!" another shouted. "We all have a right to the robe. Cut it up."

"Are you out of your mind? Cut it up? Look—it's perfect. There's not a seam in it."

"All right, then, let's roll dice for it."

And the soldiers gambled for Jesus' robe.

Above Jesus' head there was a sign that read, in three languages: KING OF THE JEWS. The chief priests, when they had seen the sign, ran back to Pilate.

"That sign should say Jesus *claimed* to be king of the Jews. He is *not* the king of the Jews."

"Get out!" Pilate shouted in anger. "What I have written, I have written!"

Jesus looked down from the cross and saw Mary, his mother, and two other women. He saw only one disciple—John. He said:

"Mother, take John with you. He will be your son now. John, take care of Mary. She is your mother now."

Other people had also surrounded the hill where Jesus was crucified.

"Save yourself, Jesus," they jeered.

Two criminals were also crucified with Jesus, one on either side of him.

"I thought you were supposed to be the Messiah," one of them said. "Well—save yourself, and us, too!"

But the other criminal answered, "Have you no decency at all? We deserve to be on these crosses. We're paying for what we did. But what has Jesus done? Jesus, remember me when you come into your kingdom."

Jesus turned his head. "I promise," he said. "You will be with me in paradise today."

Now the sky darkened as if it were night and the earth shook.

Jesus cried in a loud voice, "I have completed my work."

And with a strong sigh, Jesus died.

He Is Risen

"Y OUR Excellency," the chief priests said to Pilate, "we have another request."

"Will I never be rid of you people?" Pilate said impatiently. "What do you want?"

"Well, we remember that this Jesus said he would rise from the dead in three days."

"So? What do I care about that?"

"But—if this man's friends steal his body now and hide it, they can say that Jesus rose from the dead. Then this whole fraud would start up again."

"You people are never satisfied," Pilate said. "All right. Take some soldiers to guard the tomb. Seal the tomb. Do anything you like! Just leave me alone."

So the chief priests went and made the tomb as secure as possible and left soldiers there to guard it.

On Sunday morning, Mary Magdalene and another woman also called Mary went to visit the tomb. But as they sat outside it, the earth shook and an angel came down from heaven and rolled the great stone from the mouth of the tomb. The angel's face was as bright as a stroke of lightning.

The soldiers guarding the tomb were dazzled by the angel. They fell back and could not move. The women also were frightened.

"Don't be afraid," the angel said to the women. "I will not harm you. I know you are looking for Jesus. He is not here. He is risen from the dead. Go tell the disciples that Jesus will see them in Galilee."

The women couldn't speak. They were so happy! Jesus was risen! They ran to tell the disciples.

When the disciples heard what the women said, they couldn't

believe their ears.

"It's not possible!"

"But he's risen!"

"You must be imagining things. Your sorrow has upset your minds."

"But the angel told us! He is risen!"

Peter turned to John. "John," he said, "let's go and see for ourselves."

Peter and John ran to the tomb. John was younger and faster and reached the tomb first. But he did not go in. He could see that the tomb was empty. When Peter arrived, they both went in to the tomb. It was empty! The cloths that Jesus' body had been wrapped in were on the ground. The cloth that had covered his face was neatly folded and put in a corner.

"It's true! He is risen!"

Peter and John ran home to tell the other disciples the good news.

That same evening the disciples were all gathered together in one room. They had locked the doors and windows because they were still afraid of the Jews.

Suddenly, Jesus appeared in the middle of the room.

"Peace," he said.

He showed them his hands, where the nails had been, and his side, where a soldier had pierced him with a spear. Then he said again, "Peace."

The disciples were struck dumb. It was Jesus!

"The Father sent me to do this work," Jesus said. "Now I am sending you to continue the work." Then he breathed on them and said, "Receive the Holy Spirit. If you forgive anyone's sins, then God will consider them forgiven. If you do not forgive them, they are not forgiven."

Then Jesus disappeared.

Shortly after that, the disciple Thomas, who had not been there when Jesus had appeared, came in.

"Thomas!" the other disciples shouted. "Jesus was here. You just missed him."

"You've all gone out of your minds," Thomas said. "Small wonder. You're all huddled up here like trapped men."

"But it's true!"

"We saw him!"

"We saw his wounds!"

"We're *not* crazy."

Thomas looked at them. "You *are* crazy! Look—when I can put my finger in the wounds the nails made and in the wounds in his side, then I'll believe."

"But, Thomas!"

"You heard me. I want to touch the wounds!"

And no matter how much they tried, the disciples could not make Thomas believe they had seen Jesus.

Then, a week later, the disciples were in the room again. This time Thomas was with them.

Jesus appeared again and said:

"Peace."

Immediately he turned to Thomas. "Thomas," he said,

"come. Touch the wounds."

"Master—oh no, I . . ."

"Come. Give me your hand. I don't want you to doubt me any longer. I want you to believe in me."

And Jesus took Thomas's fingers and touched them to the wounds.

"My Lord and my God!" Thomas said.

"Thomas," Jesus said, "you believe because you can see me. Many others will not see. But they will be happy, because they will believe."

The Road to Emmaus

I JUST don't know what to think, Cleopas." Two of Jesus' disciples were walking down the road from Jerusalem to Emmaus. "We know Jesus died on the cross—and now the women say he is alive again."

"Yes, it's all so confusing. And Peter and John—they found the tomb empty. What can that mean?"

"I don't know. The whole world seems to have turned upside down."

As they were talking, another man came up beside them. It was Jesus, but his followers did not recognize him.

"What are you talking about?" Jesus asked.

"What else is there to talk about these days?" Cleopas answered.

"I don't understand," Jesus said.

"Well," the other disciple explained, "everyone is talking about the things that happened in Jerusalem these past few days."

"What things?"

"You must have heard about Jesus of Nazareth," Cleopas said. "Well, we were sure he was the Messiah. But the chief priests had him turned over to the Romans, and they crucified him."

"Yes, and then just this morning some women in our group went to the tomb and they say an angel appeared to them and said Jesus was alive."

"And—and Peter and John went to the tomb and found it empty. But they didn't see Jesus anywhere."

"You're being foolish," Jesus said.

"What?"

"Yes. Didn't you know from scriptures that the Messiah would suffer?" And Jesus explained all of the scriptures to

them.

When they were near Emmaus, Jesus acted as if he would continue walking farther down the road.

"Wait," Cleopas said. "Stay with us. It's almost evening."

"At least have supper with us."

"All right," Jesus answered.

When they were at the table, Jesus took some bread, blessed it, and gave it to the disciples.

As soon as he did this, they all recognized him. But, immediately, Jesus disappeared.

"What . . . ?" "Jesus was with us and we . . ."

"We didn't even recognize him!"

"But there was something in the way he talked. It made me feel good all over."

"Yes. But . . . but come! We have to go back to Jerusalem. We have to tell the others!"

They returned to Jerusalem, practically running the whole way. They found the other disciples and shouted happily.

"It's true! We saw Jesus! The women were right! Jesus is alive!"

Breakfast by the Sea

I'M GOING fishing," Peter said to the disciples. It was a short while after Jesus had risen from the dead. The disciples had traveled back to the Sea of Galilee. "It looks like a good night for a catch."

"We'll go with you," the other disciples said.

They pushed the boat out from shore and then sailed toward the center of the lake. They fished the whole night, but caught nothing.

At dawn they started back toward the shore. As they came closer, they noticed a man standing on the shore. It was Jesus, but they did not recognize him.

"Did you catch anything, friends?" Jesus called from the shore.

"No," they answered.

"Throw your net out on the right side of the boat. You'll find plenty there."

They shrugged their shoulders, but since they didn't have a fish in the boat, they decided to try once more.

The net had barely got into the water when it filled with fish! They could hardly get it back in the boat!

"It's Jesus," John said to Peter.

"Wha . . ." Peter immediately jumped into the water and swam to the shore. The others brought the boat in. When they got ashore, they saw that Jesus had built a fire and provided some bread.

"Bring some of the fish you just caught," Jesus said.

Peter dragged the net closer to the fire.

"Now," Jesus said, "let's have some breakfast!" And he gave them some bread and cooked the fish for them.

After breakfast, Jesus said:

"Peter, do you love me more

than the others do?"

"Why, yes, Lord. You know I love you."

"Feed my lambs."

Peter wondered what this could mean. Then Jesus asked again:

"Peter, do you love me?"

"Yes—you know I do."

"Take care of my sheep."

Peter felt confused. He could still remember—how could he forget?—how he had denied Jesus.

Jesus said again:

"Peter, do you love me?"

Peter was upset that Jesus should ask him again.

"Lord, I'm just a simple man. But you know everything. You know I really love you."

Jesus smiled. "Feed my sheep. You will have to suffer very much, Peter. But you must carry on my work."

"Yes, Lord. I will carry it on."

To the Ends of the Earth

JESUS appeared often to the disciples during the forty days that followed his resurrection. On the fortieth day he appeared to them for the last time. He took them to the Garden of Olives where he had prayed with them so often.

"Lord," they asked him, "has the time finally come? Will you become King of Israel now?"

"My Father decides things like that. You will not know the time or the day. But the Holy Spirit will come to you and you will be strong. You will preach my message to the whole world."

When he finished speaking, Jesus was lifted up toward heaven and disappeared in a cloud. As the disciples watched this, two men dressed in white suddenly appeared beside them.

"Galileans," they said, "why are you looking into the sky? Jesus has been taken to heaven—but, one day, he will return."

The disciples, stunned by what they had seen and heard, returned to Jerusalem, to the room they had so often used since Jesus had been crucified.

All the apostles were present:
Peter and John,
James and Andrew,
Philip and Thomas,
Bartholomew and Matthew,
James and Simon,
and Jude.

"You know that there were twelve apostles," Peter said. "You also know what happened to Judas. We must elect another apostle to take Judas's place."

They all discussed this and prayed about it. Finally, they nominated two men: Joseph and Matthias. Then the disciples prayed again:

"Lord, You know all things. Show us which of these two men should fill the post that Judas abandoned."

Then they drew lots, and the lot fell to Matthias and he became one of the twelve apostles.

Twelve days later, the disciples were again in the room. Suddenly the house shook. It was as if a powerful wind had blown through. Then tongues of fire came down and rested on the head of each disciple. It was the Holy Spirit.

And they were all filled with courage and strength. They left the room and began preaching in Jesus' name.

The preaching has never stopped. The words of Jesus have reached the ends of the earth!